Why do I want to do this?

A "desire to help" is not enough!

A personal story

Over thirty years ago I went to southern Africa. In apartheid Namibia I became the Principal of one of only three High Schools permitted, for Black students. At that time I had no degree, no teaching qualification, and no teaching experience. Twelve years after returning home, qualifying and getting real experience I got the UK job of the person who had sent me there – and I could not send unqualified, inexperienced people as I had been.

Thankfully, today the needs and opportunities are different.

Philip Wetherell

Preface

Working in Development is one of those rare resources – a fact-packed guide filled with practical advice and tips to help you take your first steps into International Development.

By starting your research here you will save yourself time, avoid some false steps and increase your chances of success in finding what you're looking for. If you don't yet know what you're looking for beyond a broad idea that you want to help change the world, the information here can help you become clearer about how you might do that.

The advice on applying for jobs and the comprehensive lists of websites provide in one place everything you need to get you started on the road to working in development. The useful Do's and Don'ts and some questions to prompt you to develop your own job search are invaluable.

I hope you enjoy reading it. I know you will find it really useful.

Elaine Smethurst
Manager
Working for a Charity
NCVO (National Council for Voluntary Organisations)

Index

Introduction

Introduction

From the outside, trying to find work in International Development can seem like a confusing puzzle. There is no doubt that it is complex, particularly as the opportunities and concerns are played on the global stage, and finding your place will involve resources, research, time, patience and probably some luck.

This book is divided into seven sections and each is important in understanding how you can improve your chances to get into Development work. Each section will give guidance and information to help you shape each piece of your own puzzle.

Perhaps the most important section is the first; are you the right kind of person? If you're not, then is it realistic to expect that you will change? Just like a puzzle piece, you need to be made of the right material.

In Understanding the Sector, which is vital if you want to work in it, we stress that there are three important things needed for technical assistance Development jobs – skills, commitment and personal qualities – as well as practical matters relationships or goals in your own life that might influence your decisions. Following this, there is a section on Development agencies and the general working conditions, the kind of jobs that are available, whether there is a career path, and the kind of financial and other rewards there might be.

After all that essential background information, our biggest section looks at some ways in, as we suggest various tactics and possibilities you may not have thought about. No single way is better than others, though some are more usual. We underline the value of experience and volunteering.

We then help you to analyse your skills, describe those looked for in various levels of jobs, and how to analyse what you have. This is followed by sections on training, the relevance of a Development degree and coaching.

Later sections provide practical ways to develop your skills, find how to get your name on relevant databases, discover where to look for advertised jobs and the techniques of applying including how to create a good CV and do well at interviews.

The book has been developed through hundreds of conversations at One to One consultations conducted by World Service Enquiry, in research needed for presentations at events and universities, and in answering telephone enquiries. It incorporates the data and research put together to meet these needs, answering the common questions and giving information that people want.

Some ideas and information are repeated in different sections when relevant, as this book is designed to help you at various stages in the process, rather than to be read cover-to-cover.

We hope you find Working in Development helpful in helping you to consider where you may fit in.

SECTION ONE:

Is this right for me?

A survey of graduates produced a wish-list of employers. For business students, the top three were PricewaterhouseCoopers, HSBC and the BBC; for engineers and science students, the BBC, NHS and the Environment Agency; for humanities students, the BBC, Foreign and Commonwealth Office and the Civil Service Faststream. Women had a greater feeling of the need to make a contribution rather than profit; for business students, salary and performance-related bonuses were important, but over half the total wanted a good work/life balance and one third a 'challenging job'. Around 45% saw overseas working as significant. However, only one charity featured in any list of top 10 and only for humanities students. The article concluded: *"Ethical considerations and corporate social responsibilities were also mentioned, with a large percentage of humanities and engineers, science and IT saying it was a key consideration when choosing an employer"*.[1]

Apart from business students, it is the BBC, with a good work/life balance and reasonable financial reward that people hope for although ethics were also mentioned and were for some a key consideration. Do you fit there? Or is there something else that drives you? Are ethics worth more than a mention? Does 'Development' seem the right ethical involvement for you? Whether you are a recent graduate or not, what motivated you to buy this book? Is Development work right for you?

Get Real

David Bent is a Sustainability Consultant at *Forum for the Future*. He suggests we look at career as the process of living right and gives this advice to people starting out:

■ It's good to have a vision of where you want to get to, but be flexible on how you get there;

■ Time not working is not time wasted, if afterwards you can show what you have learned and why it is relevant;

■ A career is not one job after another. Right livelihood serves people, deepens that person through continual learning experience and does both of these with as little harm to others as possible;

[1] The Guardian Newspaper 20/05/2006

- You don't need to be good at everything, but you do need to be good enough to do lots of things. Find out what you are good at (and enjoy) and find out what you need to be good enough at.[2]

In their online recruitment information, Skillshare International (www.skillshare.org) suggest that you need to answer 'yes' to all these questions before you can be considered for development work.

- Do you have the right qualifications and skills?

- Are you resourceful?

- Can you work alone or in a team?

- Are you the right age?

- Do you keep going when things are getting difficult?

- Do you know when to take a step back and take a fresh look?

- Can you adapt to a completely different culture and lifestyle?

- Do you get on well with new people?

- Can you afford to do this, financially?

- Have you talked this through with your family and friends?

- Are you really sure this is what you want to do?

"Development is about helping communities to help themselves, whether this is in Eastern Europe, Africa, Asia. Work in development does not have to be overseas. For example, in the UK you could be working with refugees, development education groups. Many would argue that you can do more for development in the South by working in the North."[3]

Where the job is situated is perhaps significant in your choice, but developed or developing world, wherever you want to be, choose to be or end up, there are common threads in finding work in Development and here is a summary to start you thinking.

Satisfying, Enjoyable and Productive – Not Always Easy

- Job satisfaction can be great. It feels good to work for something you believe in. You may make a real difference to lives, both yours and others.

- Committed colleagues will often be inspiring to work with. There are new opportunities which take in skills from outside the sector: micro-finance and IT are two obvious areas.

- Meeting new people in new cultural situations, hearing or sharing stories from around the world can be life-enhancing. Confronting world issues at ground level can be life-

---

[2] David Bent: Forum for the Future www.forumforthefuture.org.uk

[3] What is Development? From the website of the Career Development and Employment Centre of Sussex University

changing, from buying fairly-traded goods to campaigning for changes in government policy. There will often be flexibility to allow personal interests and skills to develop.

- NGOs often make a commitment to pay the market rate for support staff and may have a much lower than average pay differential between top and bottom, but if you want career certainty or a salary compatible with the commercial world, stop here. Development jobs (except at the highest level of UN/World Bank and the main director appointments of large NGOs and some fundraising jobs) are paid considerably below market rates but have other rewards. Salaries overseas may be at the local level though UK benefits will usually be preserved, so are there financial implications for you? How will you pay off your student loan, or maintain a mortgage?

- Job security is perhaps less important than in previous times and many people change jobs frequently anyway, but in this sector jobs are often dependent on government or project fund-raising which often creates uncertainities. In addition, training and skills up-dating may not be possible with smaller NGO's which will affect later job applications outside the sector.

- Many contracts are now short-term (2-3 years) so this may be something you move in and out of as circumstances and other commitments allow.

- Most jobs in development will be home-based. Many people hope to work overseas, but development agencies see the training of local staff as a priority. For example, Oxfam have a recruitment strategy labelled 'Grow your own', targeting locals and nationals. Save the Children decided in 2005 to devolve decision-making processes to national level. This has meant job cuts in London but an increased number of staff in its overseas country offices, most recruited locally.

- Most overseas placements are for single people and are in situations where there is no adequate education for children or local health care. The exceptions are at senior level and with some Christian agency sponsored appointments, where families are encouraged for the life-style example they should give.

- The main opportunities are for people with specific skills: technical (especially Engineers), Health, Education, Training, Agriculture, Logistics, Management, Finance, Fundraising, etc., and for specialists in the areas of Human Rights, Law, HIV, etc. Specific local knowledge or language skills may be required.

- Short-term possibilities are often possible for Medicine, Education and Community work. Many of these will be volunteer posts, but others will be for short-term advice or cover. Our *Guide to Volunteering for Development* [4] gives details of many agencies and NGOs looking for short-term help.

- There are common aims in all, 'caring' professions whether Social work, Healthcare or development. They attract similar kinds of people, and skills are often transferable. They all need practical people at grassroots and good management at the top. People involved at different levels may have equal commitment to political change.

- Development agencies are equally as professional in choosing people as other caring professions, but they will also be looking for different things. Many are small and so

[4] Guide to Volunteering for Development from www.wse.org.uk

may require either very generalised skills (i.e. people who can do a bit of everything) or very particular skills (e.g. if the agency specialises in legal, technical or regional issues). The field is varied, but one thing is common to all: they will want appropriate skills, but after that they will look at who you are, what you think, and particularly for overseas jobs, whether you will stay the course. And they will look for evidence of your commitment.

In summary: the personal rewards are high and there is a good chance of job satisfaction, you will be inspired by the people you meet, the issues you tackle will assist other people rather than enriching yourself. Your contribution to development will not cease on leaving a job but will have been empowering, so that the experience may change life-style, political and social views and influence how you determine to spend the rest of your life. There are many ways to begin your journey, and many ideas follow later on.

Who Are You?

Paul Kingsnorth, an ethical journalist, claims that each year 50% of all graduates want to get into writing or journalism. Most, he says, will follow "well-worn career paths". He adds "You will be strongly advised to do the same. My advice: Don't. This is a way to lose your soul". Instead he suggests:

- set your priorities (do what you really want to do);

- be prepared to be financially poor for a while (getting on the housing ladder is not essential);

- think about getting useful experience (work experience to broaden your knowledge of the world). This may be specially important for journalists who have to write about it, but can be also important for anyone who has led a relatively protected life;

- keep your eye on the prize: "Whatever you end up doing, remember why you're doing it".

He concludes: "You only get one life – don't sell it to someone else; make the most of it".[5]

Working for a Charity at NCVO (National Council for Voluntary Organisations) has useful online information and runs a short course on getting into the charity sector, which is a good way of assessing whether this is right for you. www.workingforacharity.org.uk.

Another alternative is The University of Liverpool's Windmills Programme that helps you to look at autonomy/enterprise, stability, sense of purpose, balanced lifestyle, reward/authority, expertise and challenge and then asks you how important each of these is to you. Further details at www.windmillsonline.co.uk.

Ann Mold, a career coach and therapist[6], has suggested using a 'Wheel of Life' to help see what kind of career would be right to enable your correct work/life balance for you. (See appendix A)

---

[5] Paul Kingsnorth on Ethical Journalism. The Alternative Careers Fair Handbook 2007 www.careers.ox.ac.uk

[6] www.changebychoice.co.uk

Values

Am I the person wanted by overseas NGOs?

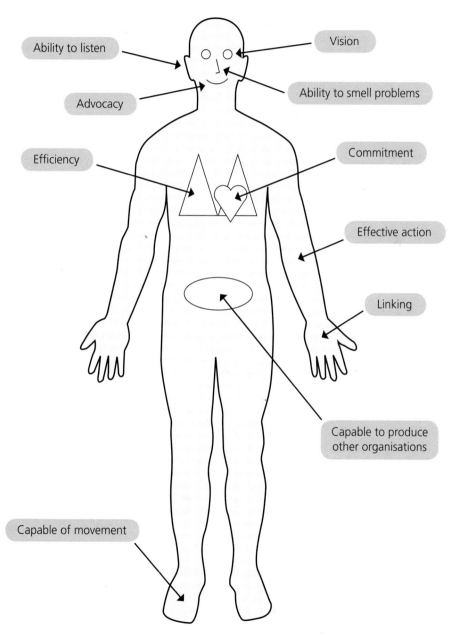

Ability to listen

Vision

Advocacy

Ability to smell problems

Efficiency

Commitment

Effective action

Linking

Capable to produce other organisations

Capable of movement

Adapted 'NGO Mache' tool from a Nepalese NGO's training material.
This suggests what organisations and NGO people need to be like.

Hopefully this process will have clarified your commitment. But for confirmation, ask yourself again, "Why do I want to work in development?"

■ Personal satisfaction? *(But what satisfies me?)*

■ Doing good? *(Is this the best way to do it using my skills?)*

■ Helping the poor? *(Do they want my help; who says they want help; how is that best done?)*

■ Ending injustice? *(Why don't I get into politics, where policy change has to happen for real change in the developing world?)*

■ Want to travel, and gain new experiences? *(Is that enough?)*

■ Money? *(65% of advertised jobs are at less than £20k p.a.)*

■ Job security? *(Fairly unlikely)*

■ Fame? *(Probably only if I am already a pop star or involved in a media-attracting international incident)*

So, ask yourself:

Is this right for me?

Will I fit in?

What kind of person am I?

What is important to me?

What am I looking for?

If you are sure that this is right for you, what will help you to learn about the sector?

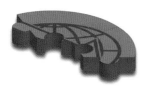

SECTION TWO:
The Sector – What Do I Need To Know?

If you come near to the kind of person portrayed in that image from Nepal then the Development sector needs you. In addition to being the kind of person they are looking for, you need to understand current trends and issues in the sector, how agencies work and what else they are looking for.

Terminology in Recruitment

The Development sector, like any other specialism, has its own jargon. People from the private or public sectors entering the Development sector may take time to learn the language and the acronyms. Some of the common terminology associated with agencies is explained below, though many organisations don't fit neatly into just one category.

NGO
> A Non Governmental Organisation, often committed to a particular cause – may not be a registered charity if it has a political stance.

IGO
> Inter-Governmental Organisation – such as the World Trade Organisation (WTO).

NFP
> Not for profit – often used in the USA for NGO, but can include commercially-based agencies.

Third Sector
> Another name used for the not for profit, voluntary or charity sector.

Charity
> Recognised under national law as for the benefit of others – in the UK must be registered with Charity Commission (www.charity-commission.gov.uk) or Scottish equivalent (www.oscr.org.uk).

DFID
> The Department for International Development of the UK Government.

BOND
> The umbrella group British Overseas NGOs for Development.

MDG

Millennium Development Goals; the target for development agencies and nations.

Volunteer

Unpaid work, full- or part-time, although travel and lunch expenses are normally given. In overseas placements this usually means self-funded except possibly for accommodation. Note: Despite its name VSO (Voluntary Service Overseas) is not a volunteer agency.

Internship

Guided work placement of limited duration and reward. Inside the USA internships are really voluntary work but can count towards a degree. Elsewhere it is usually a post-graduate opportunity to gain experience, usually low-paid, if at all.

Relief or Aid work

Short-term in response to a natural or man-made emergency. With no time for adjustment, training or learning on the job, people who are known to have existing skills will be brought in – water engineers (water being the essential to prevent malnutrition and disease), logisticians (for the supply of aid), those with relevant health care experience and possibly local language skills. Most major agencies have a register of such people known to them who are able to leave their present job at short notice.

Aid

Often used as another term for Development but for many outside the sector, aid is seen as longer-term financial, food or other direct support rather than changes in systems, politics or trade terms.

Development

Concentrates on long-term projects to strengthen local economies or structures. On a large scale it is often related to international targets or government funding priorities.

More can be found on many websites including the UK government's Department for International Development; www.dfid.gov.uk/aboutdfid/glossary.asp

Working for a Charity (www.workingforacharity.org.uk) exists to promote the voluntary sector as a positive career option for those seeking paid employment and to promote the opportunities and benefits of becoming a volunteer to people who wish to do unpaid work. Their website has very informative content about many aspects of the voluntary sector.

More on the jargon used in the voluntary sector (as opposed to that specifically for development), can be found on www.volresource.org.uk/moreres/glossary.htm Another site, with a downloadable book 'Working for Charities' is www.cfappointments.com, which also has general information on the history and legal framework of the charity sector.

The Trends

Partly in response to government policy, NGOs are strengthening local country offices, often with local staff or expertise and stressing the partnerships that are being created with local agencies or governments. There is also evidence of a shift towards internationalisation at top level. Local staff cost less (no air fares, expensive insurance or other home support) and know the local culture and language. Success in Development inevitably means fewer jobs for external experts, e.g. ActionAid has a staff of 2,000 and only 35 expatriates.

- New expertise is needed particularly in business development, technical skills, micro-finance, and those able to train and support locally-appointed staff.

- There is more professionalism too, often bringing in expertise and policy ideas from outside the sector, e.g. in human resources, public health, accountancy and fundraising.

- A wider variety of people are now involved in decision-making. Directors and volunteers, the two ends of the small NGO sector, and the stakeholders all have influence.

- Response to disasters and success of campaigns, or the input from celebrities can shift emphases and jobs within the sector. For example the response to the 2004/5 Tsunami affected later funding for other work and agencies. Causes now supported by the Princess Diana Memorial Fund (land-mine removal and casualties) previously had far less prominence. Some advocacy groups such as Jubilee 2000, Make Poverty History and successor groups can exert considerable influence. These include faith-based groups as well as secular agencies.

- Governments are more proactive. For example, in the UK, programmes wanting government funding often have to relate to the Millennium Development Goals or other criteria.

- Block grants, such as the Partnership Programme of DFID, etc., now often favour larger NGOs. Project Funding is often short-term and can mean that NGOs have to gear work and funding requests to funders' priorities rather than their own. This can mean short-term appointments and insecurity in the workplace.

- Fixed- and shorter-term employment contracts. UK/EU law says there is no liability to pay redundancy if the contract is less than two years. Within the sector funding is often uncertain.

The Issues

It will help to know some more about the sector, the words used, the current issues you might be asked about in interview or can refer to in applications, particularly if you are not an expert or a recent graduate in development studies.

> *So what is the Cotonou Agreement, what has it to do with Lomé; why is the ACP involved and how did it result in an EPA?*

Don't know? Then learn the jargon and stay acquainted with the key issues; show them you are not just a naïve 'do gooder'; keep up to date.

- Keep abreast of changes in government policy and strategy: www.dfid.gov.uk and www.fco.gov.uk for UK government policy on development and (FCO) on policy towards individual countries. The Foreign and Commonwealth Office (FCO) site will send up-dates on policy, ministers' speeches, etc. www.fco.gov.uk.

- www.ids.ac.uk, www.eldis.org, are good for wider policy discussions – the last having frequent up-dates and printable papers on current issues. The Eldis Resource Guides cover 30 topics including Aging, to Conflict, Food Security, Information and Communication Technology for Development to, and World Bank.

- If you are very new to the development sector try www.bized.ac.uk and their 'virtual world'. In a virtual country (Zambia, in fact) they explore issues as varied as trade policy, debt, agriculture and aid, with case studies produced by NGOs on subjects such as whether microfinance will change the future of a shanty town.

- If you prefer reading books, you may enjoy the New Internationalist series of No-Nonsense Guides, whose titles include *International Development*.

Be aware of current campaigns. A web search will give a variety of opinions on these, as will the links from independent websites: www.globalpolicy.org, www.oneworld.net and www.ips.org. Know what major international agencies are saying in your particular area of concern.

World Bank	www.worldbank.org
International Monetary Fund	www.imf.org
International Labour Organisation	www.ilo.org
World Health Organisation	www.who.int
World Trade Organisation	www.wto.org
United Nations sites	www.undp.org (development programme) www.who.int (health) www.fao.org (food and agriculture)
Human Rights Watch	www.hrw.org
UK Government policy	www.dfid.org.uk (overseas development) www.fco.gov.uk (foreign policy)

Subscribe at www.developments.org.uk to the free quarterly DFID magazine *Developments*, or subscribe to the *New Internationalist* (www.newint.org).

BOND (British Overseas NGOs for Development) has a website that allows you to monitor and keep up to date: www.bond.org.uk/policy/monitorself.html.

For practical information get on AidWorkers, www.aidworkers.net, a web based forum for development and humanitarian professionals. Many development and aid workers now keep online journals called web logs, or blogs. You can read some blogs about people working in relief and development on Aid Workers Network.

Find and read local newspapers on the net, such as www.world-newspapers.com, www.onlinenewspapers.com and check the BBC site www.news.bbc.co.uk and click on 'world'.

Find out about the agencies you are interested in applying to on both their own website and through the Charity Commission (www.charity-commission.gov.uk) and Guidestar (www.guidestar.org.uk).

Many Different Agencies

What do they want from you and how do they work?

The greatest numbers of agencies working overseas in development are NGOs, which have their own distinctive culture and a variety of approaches. Many agencies work in partnership with an overseas government, organisation, network or community. In theory, the overseas partners indicate what they need and consider to be beneficial to their community, though some 'aid', its finance and staff can be determined by powerful donors.

Development Agency

A development agency is committed to long-term projects, contributing to improving the welfare of a community through funding or other support. Current policy is towards helping developing countries help themselves through providing expert guidance, so the emphasis is on training local staff to carry out the work after the development worker leaves. Agencies provide technical and vocational expertise that developing countries could not afford if they were paying the commercial rate. Development is intended to lead to a strengthening of infra-structures, hopefully enabling effective and appropriate responses to minor problems that could otherwise become disasters. Most development agencies work with projects that are managed by local people and don't need outside expertise. Some agencies may recruit qualified and experienced personnel to contribute to creating local employment, better health, better education or generally helping set in motion a process of improvement. The need is for skilled people who are able to adapt their skills to different circumstances, with personal qualities being extremely important.

As explained previously, the majority of jobs are now home-based, with most people employed in support work, publicity, promotion, fundraising, finance, policy making and research. Expatriate staff are increasingly not the rule but rather the exception and are only appointed when local expertise is unavailable. Today, a development worker seeking work will find s/he is in a highly competitive arena with candidates applying from all over the world in a truly global job market. Work permit regulations at both ends can influence who gets which job.

A DFID policy analyst has written of a *"glimpse into a different side of the Civil Service"*:

"As a donor agency, DFID provides both funding and technical support to developing country Governments and civil society organisations in support of poverty reduction and achievement of the Millennium Development Goals. The type of jobs DFID offers vary from advisory positions (in the area of economics, governance, social development, health, infrastructure and statistics) to programme management of a country programme, and policy based work on issues including the effectiveness of aid, economic growth, health and sustainable development. DFID also has an entire division dedicated to the international system (by which we mean the UN system, World Bank and other international financial institutions, as well as trade reform). And not forgetting that as a Government department there are

also core teams dedicated to the parliamentary business of the department in support of our two Ministers. In a nutshell, the first really positive factor about working in DFID is the immense variety of work, both in our UK offices and overseas... However, it's important to be realistic about the type of work; working in a donor agency in 2006 is no longer simply about digging wells in poor communities. In fact the traditional project is less common in DFID's work than twenty years ago due to its focus on working towards country led sustainable development... This is a positive shift, but it does mean that you will spend more time at policy tables working with (or to influence) key partners in the development process, and less time in 'the field'. Therefore, you can sometimes feel slightly separated from the 'poor' and do increasingly less direct work with local people than many NGOs. It also means there are less visible 'quick wins' (in that you don't immediately see the school that has been built) but instead you work towards longer term development strategies being out into place".[7]

Aid Agency

An aid agency primarily raises funds for its overseas partner activities and provides support and occasionally expertise for long-term projects. Many aid agencies are involved in emergency relief and development work. Staff are occasionally recruited to work overseas and there is strong competition for any job that may arise within headquarters. If such a job does appear, it will often require substantial overseas experience, country or even regional knowledge, appropriate language, and ability to relate to other donors. As with most agencies, the majority of jobs will be home-based and in such areas as: administration, advocacy, promotion, finance, fundraising, etc.

Relief Agency

A relief agency carries out immediate operations to alleviate the effects of a disaster on a population. The effects of natural disasters are aggravated by conditions of poverty and underdevelopment and therefore have more serious consequences for a poor community, which often has less resilience and fewer local resources. Relief workers are required at short notice for short periods of time and in most cases have worked in a relief situation before. They are usually placed overseas for a few weeks or months. If you have a relevant skill and the personal resilience to contribute to a relief situation, you need to be pre-registered with a relief agency in preparation for an emergency, and in a regular job that allows you to take leave at short notice.

Emergency relief roles are often highly specialised. The skills most required for disaster relief include engineering (often to do with water supply, sanitation, or road-building and construction), logistics (to get things in the right place at the right time) and medical (surgical, tropical health, etc.). Some of these skills might often be found in ex-military personnel.

[7] Nicolette Stoddart, Policy Analyst, DFID

Faith-based Agencies

Historically, the UK has a long tradition of Christian faith-based agencies, (USPG for example can trace their roots back to 1701), that sent school teachers and clerics overseas to colonies. Today, the world is a very different place, and many faith-based agencies continue to send people overseas and they often deal with potential candidates in a different way from the other development agencies. Many will interview without advertising a specific job and then fit skills to known opportunities, and this therefore expects an openness to suggestions of regions or work you might not have anticipated. This would be particularly true of those in education, health or social work where the agency has a number of vacancies. Personal faith in sympathy with that of the sending agency and agreement to work alongside the local faith-based community are important in the selection process. Other agencies, such as Christian Aid, will not necessarily require a faith commitment for specific emergency or relief jobs.

The key point is that some Christian agency, 'Development' jobs are distinguishable from the evangelising or ministerial posts, which we are not dealing with here. However, some agencies will not make that distinction, thus opening themselves to the suggestion that their development work is simply a device of their conversion aim. Their answer will be that one encourages the other.

The majority of jobs are in health and education but there are also opportunities in administration, AIDS/HIV work in church-run hospitals and clinics, agriculture, training and other roles. In the UK the majority of these agencies are Christian based and Christians Abroad (www.cabroad.org.uk) can give individuals advice on the way to proceed.

Most agencies expect their candidates to finance their own posting while overseas, and expect family and home churches to support them. This has a risk factor if such support is not maintained.

Advice and help across the whole Christian sector (and some jobs) can be found through the ecumenical CTBI agency Christians Abroad (www.cabroad.org.uk). Christian Aid is the biggest Christian aid agency (www.christian-aid.org); the Catholic Missionary Union brings together Roman Catholic agencies, but many posts are limited to members of religious orders (www.cmu.org.uk). It is also worth looking at www.cafod.org.uk and www.progressio.org.uk. Christian Vocations' online database (www.christianvocations.org) has overseas positions with evangelical Christian organisations working worldwide, including tent-making opportunities (jobs which earn income from other sources to enable 'Christian' work to be done alongside, sometimes in situations where 'evangelism' is the main aim but perhaps not permitted in the local situation). There are many other Christian based agencies including, the World Council of Churches, Renovabis, Kirche in Not, the Lutheran World Federation, International Orthodox Christian Charities, etc. that work in humanitarian aid and development among people irrespective of their confessional identity.

While the majority of the United Kingdom's faith-based agencies are Christian there are possibilities for members of other faiths – although the job and volunteer opportunities in the UK are limited – through a range of other faith based agencies.

Islamic relief agencies came into greater prominence and took the lead at the time of the 2005 Pakistan earthquake. Muslim aid, www.muslimaid.org, founded in 1985 in London by 23 leading British Muslim organisations in response to continuing conflicts and disasters around the world, looks for volunteers in its London office as well as having wider connections. Islamic Relief, www.islamic-relief.com, founded in 1984 promotes sustainable economic and social development by working with local communities through relief and development programmes. Islamic Aid, www.islamicaid.org.uk, seeks to make immediate and lasting improvements to the lives of people affected by poverty, war and disaster and rarely recruits.

Sewa International is a Hindu agency that is run by volunteers and a service project of Hindu Swayamsevak Sangh (www.sewainternational.com). Hindu Aid coordinates and facilitates the aid and development work of Hindu organisations in the United Kingdom. It is the premiere Hindu organisation that provides Development Education training aimed towards British Hindus (www.hinduaid.org).

World Jewish Relief is the main charity to channel the UK Jewish community's response to disasters and need affecting the international community regardless of race, religion or nationality (www.worldjewishrelief.org.uk).

All the major faiths share a fundamental basic belief in helping others at a time of need.

Academic

A limited number of research jobs are advertised at many levels – from grassroots to government policy. The former is difficult to fund unless project-led but it may be possible through an internship. A specialist higher level degree is obviously relevant here, especially if in a university post. Development Education and advocacy jobs are important for widening public awareness through Development Education Centres and in jobs attached to larger agencies. These raise awareness of development issues, but may be linked with other campaigning and, in smaller agencies possibly, with fundraising too. These may require some experience of grass roots development work, or of a region of the world. Visit www.dea.org.uk for the Development Education Association.

Know What NGOs Are Looking For

All employers look for the person with the right skills, who will also fit the person specification. But NGOs look for something more, particularly for overseas jobs, where a mistaken appointment can put back a planned project and also incur huge financial cost. If you have to come home before your contract is completed there will be a personal cost too in practical matters such as finding a house and a job, but mostly in loss of self-esteem.

Most jobs are at UK national HQ level, but they are still looking for something more and getting a job in Development has been described as being able to sit on a stool with three legs – the three essentials.

- Skills
- Commitment
- Evidence

Skills

- Specialist or technical needed for the job: Engineering, Management, Accountancy, etc.

- People skills: team working, communication skills, training, negotiating, etc.

- Practical: basic finance and book-keeping often needed for projects; first aid; vehicle maintenance; electrical skills, etc.

- In the UK and increasingly overseas: project management and fund-raising are often needed.

- Language skills: French and Arabic are common, and a proven ability in learning any second language means you can learn others.

- Qualifications show competence and are often required for overseas work permits as well as showing your abilities.

- Experience (not a skill itself, but proof that you can use your skills).

For more on the skills needed and on developing skills see section 5; for putting these into a portfolio see section 6.

Commitment

- Evidence of previous commitment to issues, campaigns, fund-raising, parliamentary lobbying, membership of organisations, etc. is often proven through volunteering.

- An interest or concern for issues is not enough. What have you done about them?

Evidence you can cope

These are your personal qualities or soft skills. The following will help to show this:

- Experience of coping with limited resources.

- Independent living.

- Experience and/or knowledge of the developing world may be through travel, volunteering, study.

- Cross-cultural awareness shown by experience of exposure to, or engagement with other cultures in the UK; travel experience (not as a tourist).

- Absence of one-sided political or religious views affecting your acceptance of difference (e.g. views on use of condoms in HIV prevention).

- Flexibility and adaptability.

There may also be practical matters:

- Health: long-term health issues, disability, problems with heat/cold/altitude, phobias, etc.

- Family/dependants: will separation be difficult? How will you relate to partner/ children/ parents?

- Financial: what ongoing commitments do you have?

- Faith: some NGOs will require evidence of faith commitment, and it may require a certain view within that faith.

Now you know about yourself, and the sector. But what kind of work is there?

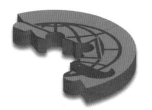

SECTION THREE:
What Kind Of Work Is There?

Details of the variety of agencies are in Section 2. Here, we deal more specifically with the kind of jobs there could be for you. Not all charities are in the development sector, but there are 180,000 registered charities. While 85% of UK charities have an income of less than £10,000 and therefore no jobs, that leaves 27,000 plus possible employers in the UK alone.[8] Of those:

20 have an income in excess of £100m
159 have an income between £20m - £100m
170 have an income between £10m - £20m
2,000 have an income between £1m - £10m
24,660 have an income between £10k - £1m

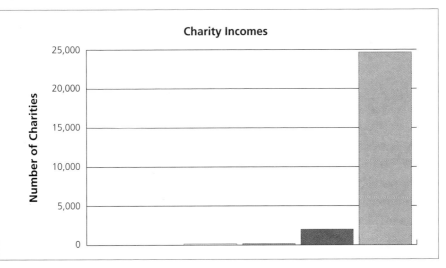

	£100m+	£20m - £100m	£10m - £20m	£1m - £10m	£10k - £1m
Total Charities	20	159	170	2,000	24,660

---

[8] The Charity Commission

The Overall Picture

Disasters are not the time for you to offer unskilled help, and dealing with inappropriate offers can distract agency staff from their main tasks. At the time of the 2005 SE Asia tsunami, World Service Enquiry had a phone call every ten minutes and up to 1,700 people per day looked at a specially compiled web page – time is money!

Education and health are two areas in which it is possible to enter after two years' UK experience or perhaps less in some circumstances. VSO, the largest person-sending NGO in the UK, has 40% (its largest number) in education. Teaching English after a four week TEFL Certificate course is perhaps the easiest route of all in terms of gaining worthwhile experience, though preferably not through commercially-run language schools.

Development programmes aim to improve (i.e. develop) Health, Education, income generation, capacity building, etc. in 'developing' countries and often include training of local people. Specific skills and experience are needed. Many small NGOs are focussed on an issue or a region or country and will look for specific knowledge and experience, plus, if very small, more general skills to help run the enterprise. Other areas are 'advisory' and 'executive', broad categories that include administration and project management, and 'technical' jobs related to very specific skills in anything from Engineering and Accountancy to aeronautics and laboratory sciences.

The majority of jobs will be home-based. As local expertise overseas is developed and governments become stricter about granting work permits to foreign nationals, the number of 'first-level' overseas jobs decreases.

In a Charity Jobs survey[9], there were 107 quoted salary jobs, of which 84 were in the UK and 66 of these were in London. In January 2007 figures were similar; 138 jobs, of which 108 were in the UK and 70 of them were in London (more detail below under 'Salaries'). In larger NGOs, there will be the head of the organisation, commonly known as the Chief Executive or General Secretary, under whom there will be the usual range of departments and jobs including; Accounts, Fundraising, IT, Department and Project Managers, specialist Country Officers and Administrators, Sales and Marketing, Human Resources, Training. In larger organisations you may find separate departments for Campaigns, Advocacy, Public Enquiries, Press Office, Post Room, Help-Desk or Reception staff. In smaller NGOs, people will 'multi-task' which is one way of learning skills.

A breakdown of jobs calculated from three recent issues of *Opportunities Abroad*[10] showed the following:

Management (35)	Church work (19)	Health (87)
Administration (123)	Communications (9)	Social/Community (12)
Agriculture (13)	Education (46)	Technical (29)

An average of 60 agencies advertised an average of 372 jobs. Under Administration will be everything from project management and accountancy to human resources and disaster management.

[9] Carried out by us

[10] World Service Enquiry's monthly job magazine see www.wse.org.uk

The development work database on www.dev-zone.org groups the kind of jobs currently available. Recently, in one month there were 470 jobs. The categories used are chosen by the advertiser and some allowance may need to be made for that, with jobs perhaps 'labelled' above their real status. They are listed in order here, the largest number being in:

- Health (32)
- Education (30)
- Management (28)
- Community development (27)

With the exception of Management these would be the easiest areas to enter at a low entry level. There were 21 volunteer/internship opportunities, and other areas with a similar number were:

- Capacity building (22)
- Administration (20)
- Agriculture/Rural Development (20)
- Economics/Finance (20)
- Social Development (18)
- Monitoring and Evaluation (18)
- Business Development (18)

The only others getting into double figures were:

- Human Rights (12)
- Environment (11)
- Governance (11)
- Resource Management (10)

The other areas were:

- Civil Society and Water/Sanitation (9)
- Poverty and Engineering (8)
- Training and Trade (7)
- Disaster/Emergency management, Information Management, Policy, Advocacy/Campaigns and Research (6)
- Energy, Communications/Media, and Marketing (5)
- Population, Food, and Peace/Conflict (4)
- Law, Gender (3)
- Logistics, Science, Tourism and Youth (2)

A further 19 jobs did not fit any of their categories.

Obviously, advertised jobs will vary from month to month, but from those listed it is clear that in overseas jobs the jobs are not where some people would like them to be. Health and education are the major exceptions, but the major areas are administrative and managerial, with the very practical jobs fewer in number than many would hope for. In one sense this is good news – it means that development agencies are successfully training and employing local staff at this level.

Fundraising is increasingly important to many NGOs as core funding declines and project funding is in greater demand; It is often well-paid. Careers can be developed here and skills can be transferred to or from marketing and advocacy.

Another way to get involved and show commitment is to get into NGO or charity management as a trustee (often advertised in *The Guardian* and on www.charityjob. co.uk). The governing body of a charity is often made up of individuals known as Trustees and collectively as the Management Committee. This involvement gives signs of commitment and can provide useful networking opportunities.

A Career Path?

Within many charities and NGOs there is no set career path. Some would say there is no real career, since many development jobs are linked to project funding and may mean fixed term contracts – two or three years particularly for overseas jobs. As a consequence, it may be necessary to pursue different options in between jobs to boost skills or acquire further qualifications.

In medicine, law, IT and other rapidly changing professions it may be vital to work in a developed country in between assignments in order to keep up-to-date or maintain registration with a relevant professional body. The lack of funds for training and short contracts in many NGOs means that there is often little opportunity for continuous professional development. On the other hand more experienced people with training in older techniques and knowledge of older practices can be useful in poorer parts of the world (e.g. in medicine, where modern drugs or techniques may not be known or affordable).

David Bent says that *"a career is not one job after another"*. When leaving college Bent wanted security in a profession so he joined PricewaterhouseCoopers, (a favourite choice of Business students), where he learned skills and earned credibility. Under-stimulated by the work, he started up sustainability charities and became an environmental accountant with Forum for the Future. In many ways his story is a classic example of how to move into the sector but he also adds, *"The NGO world is great, but no organisation is large enough to have a career path"*.[11]

An article in BOND's regular magazine[12] suggests many specialists leave to become consultants as the only way to move upwards in this sector. The article goes on to discuss developing a support system for workforce development, but the reality is that this is unlikely except in the largest NGOs. There is nothing to stop anyone setting up as a consultant, but clearly you have to prove your relevance and sell yourself to 'customers'. A degree/qualification proves one competency but experience is important. The trend is increasingly to use private sector consultants in such things as encouraging local people to accept water privatisation, as the Government did in Tanzania.

---

[11] David Bent: Forum for the Future www.forumforthefuture.org.uk

[12] BOND The Networker

One way to develop a career is to move into work linked to the sector (e.g. government or 'not for profit' agencies servicing the sector). These agencies will often encourage and provide training or other personal development and this enables you to move back into direct NGO management at a higher level or in a specific skill area. Skills are acquired over years and can be collected outside the sector as well as within.

This is particularly relevant because most senior level jobs in larger NGOs will be at management rather than practitioner level and many will be at HQ. Smaller NGOs often need people with a variety of skills and too much specialism may take you out of their job range or affordability. However, small specialist NGOs will welcome developed skills even if they cannot add to them.

Salaries

Two years ago a survey of jobs advertised on the Charity Job website listed 155 in development, 107 of which carried a stated salary. 16% were over £30k, of which two thirds were in fund-raising and finance jobs, and one chief director's job of an agency 'servicing the sector' through recruitment. These 'service' jobs are often better paid than jobs truly within the sector. 10% of job offers, of which half were in fund-raising, were between £25,000 and £29,000, and 16% between £20,000 and £25,000, of which none were in fundraising. 58% of jobs had salaries of less than £20,000.

In January 2007 the situation was rather different. Of 138 jobs in development, 22% were overseas, most with no stated salary. This could be because additional benefits (housing, etc) are offered or because a local salary would be paid, which would mean little in exact transfer to developed country currencies. Of the 81 with a stated salary, 86% were in London. 23% were over £30,000, of which half were in fundraising; 35% of jobs had salaries between £25,000 and £29,000 and nearly two-thirds of these were in fundraising; and 21% had salaries between £20,000 and £24,000 with only 2 in fundraising. There were only 7 jobs or 8% where the stated salary was below £20,000 compared with 58% two years before, which perhaps suggests that salaries are rising. Across the whole charity sector (and not just development) there were 784 jobs, of which 354 were in fundraising or similar positions. (See www.charityjob.co.uk).

So, you know something about yourself, the sector and jobs, so how do you get into it?

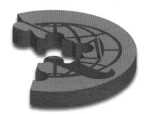

SECTION FOUR:
Ways In –
What Will Help?

Here are six real examples of how UK and overseas experience helped some people, often leading to UK higher level jobs. These are followed by ten suggestions on action you can take to help, most of which relate to experience or possibilities in the UK.

Six Examples

- A language graduate who had an overseas placement helping teachers of English, used that experience to work for a travel company and also to organise a charity 'challenge' event. After becoming disillusioned with the travel business, their free-time was used mentoring children and studying part-time for a MSc in Global Development. This led to a job at Save the Children.

- An Infant school teacher in the UK became a private language teacher in Italy and returned to the UK to become part of a volunteer group working in the community. This led to becoming head of that programme and responsible for a wider youth and volunteer programme. Personnel skills allowed a sideways move to become regional desk officer for part of Africa which in turn led to promotion in another agency and the responsibility for world-wide recruitment.

- An Economics graduate worked for a bank and while skills were enhanced, their growing desire was to work in development. An MSc in Development was followed by an ODI fellowship in Fiji looking at economic issues and then a job with DFID where their skills in economics were valued more than development knowledge.

- A VSO worker in Bangladesh became a Development Education and Community volunteer, and moved to Development Education and Child Participation Advisor with Plan UK working both here and overseas. With the same organisation there were opportunities as a support teacher for asylum seekers and refugee children, and in a variety of projects on a consultancy basis. As confidence grew, a change was made to freelance work, offering pre-departure training.

- A Sociology graduate spent a sabbatical as an Education Officer, then as a Finance Officer with the college's Student Union. A post-graduate Diploma in Self-Development, followed by time volunteering in an Oxfam shop led to an appointment as shop manager, and later as the Volunteer Placement Development Officer at Oxfam's headquarters.

- A trained nurse worked for ten years in various UK jobs, and then took 18 months out as a VSO Nurse Tutor in Tanzania. On return to the UK the previous work was resumed, mostly as Theatre Nurse, and this was followed by work with the Winged Fellowship Trust. This in turn led to becoming Head of Care for the Trust.

Ten Suggestions

Few people have the right mixture of skills, commitment and experience to move straight from college into the kind of job they yearn for in development. Some examples of the way individuals have done it are given above, but there are many more ways in, and these are expanded in this section. No single way is advised more than another, though developing and transferring a skill is perhaps the most common. It depends on you, your skills and sometimes on chance, but what is common to all is the need to demonstrate skills, prove commitment and show you have learned about the sector or a particular country or type of activity. They are not mutually exclusive, as they will also work collectively.

SUGGESTION ONE – Start Small

Starting small means volunteering or working in a small NGO. The majority with paid staff have an income of between £10k and £1m. This means that very few small agencies have specialised staff for each required function and a variety of tasks have to be done by each employee. Helping to run the organisation may give you opportunities to practise or develop many skills, and prove your flexibility.

You may be expected to use your initiative and while there you will be given a main designated task, and you may be given responsibility in more than one area of work. You will probably be involved in collective decision making, while in a larger organisation you might be very much the junior – more limited in tasks, consulted or trusted less and with fewer chances to try out a range of skills. Greater variety may also mean less boredom. The skills you use or acquire and the responsibilities can all be emphasised when you come to writing your CV to meet the person specification. This type of experience will help you to find out what you enjoy doing or have a talent for, (this may bring surprises) and it will also help you meet people, share ideas, and make contacts. More of this in suggestion four – Networking.

Simona Santojanni, the Development Officer for 'Lawyers for Liberty' writes of her post:

> *"I am a Development Officer and my main purpose is recruiting members, in particular lawyers. There's no daily routine at Liberty; one day I might be busy arranging a talk, another day I might have to think of an event, and some other time there are new members to be registered or maybe a piece needs to be written for our newsletter. Every day is different. Furthermore, both staff and volunteers are genuinely interested in the subject treated and this makes the organisation a really pleasing place to work for".*

In my own job with an NGO 50% of the job is to recruit, prepare volunteers and professionals for development work and 20% to give career advice.[13] I also have to

---

[13] see *One to One* Interviews on www.wse.org.uk

keep accounts, make budgets, raise funds, recruit office volunteers, organise health and National Insurance for overseas volunteers, make criminal records checks for other agencies, maintain office procedures, arrange and run conferences, prepare agendas and minute meetings, make overseas project visits, write newsletters, write and revise website material, handle telephone enquiries, negotiate with advertisers, attend careers fairs, formulate policies with trustees, encourage supporters, and write annual reports for Companies House and the Charity Commissioners and write this text!

It would not be sensible for me to apply to a large NGO, for something that stood alone in that list (such as Finance Officer), but in moving to another job I could group together the skills used (e.g. accuracy through keeping accounts), or the qualities they required (e.g. patience in dealing with telephone enquiries). Those used in the central part of the job such as listening and keeping confidences could be grouped together and emphasised as people skills.

In some small to medium-sized NGOs, you may get a higher profile than you would working as part of a team. For example, as the Director of Fundraising (even if it takes only 20% of your time in a small NGO) you would attend conferences and have contact with people heading large fundraising departments in larger NGOs. This is a good way to get yourself known and find out if this is a future specialised career option. You may also get training, and benefit from networking.

SUGGESTION TWO – Develop a Transferable Skill

Perhaps the best way to make a useful contribution to development, apart from changing the world through political involvement, is first to become proficient at something outside the sector and then transfer those skills. Backing that up are the following two quotes:

> *"A large percentage of our candidates are from the private sector. It depends on your experience and the positions you are interested in. However if you have a strong background of experience in your field, along with a flexible attitude it is very possible".*
>
> *"Work experience outside the charity sector is a good preparation for working in charities. Some would argue that no-one should contemplate a charity career if they have never had any other form of paid employment to acquire basic work skills and a broader experience of life. A person with good qualifications and outside experience may be more useful than someone with just enthusiasm".*[14]

The majority of development jobs need the same skills as commerce or industry. While it might not help to work for a multinational denounced by development agencies, it shows a good conscience if you leave or look for an alternative. Most employment provides experience, develops skills, provides training and helps to prove your competency. If you hope to run an overseas project or manage a programme in the UK, then experience in managing people, relating to other organisations and some budgeting and finance skills would be required. A job in the not for profit sector, in local government or a health service trust would be a useful introduction.

[14] Working for Charities. CFAppointments 4th edition 2002

Experience is vital. Common to many of the other suggested ways in is experience which demonstrates that skills have been used, proves commitment and shows that you have learned about the sector or a particular country or type of activity. One job advertisement for Oxfam mentioned experience or 'proven capabilities' 10 times in 18 'key competencies' required for a Programme Development Manager job. For Oxfam, evidence of using skills, as well as showing you know the sector and the issues facing it, were important, all factors mentioned already in section two.

Section five shows how to recognise your skills and develop them and as already suggested, this can be done successfully outside the sector.

- A classic example is in the growing area of microfinance, helping to finance and support growing small industries in developing countries, (www.microfinancegateway. org is a good source for current jobs). It is virtually impossible to get a good job in the area of finance without relevant qualifications and experience.

- An obvious area is medicine – probably the easiest area to transfer to development work overseas at a relatively inexperienced level. However, you still have to be qualified and recognised within your expertise, such as nursing, surgery, physiotherapy, etc. A further specialism such as tropical health clearly helps for working in the tropics.

- A third example is fundraising, which is currently the highest paid part of the sector. You do need to learn about the area, but if you have proven skills in UK charity or corporate fundraising these are easily transferred to the development world. Less immediately obvious but important in a sector short on funding are effective management and strategic planning skills.

- Managing volunteers, negotiating with or reporting to donors, legal skills (for Human Rights NGOs etc.), Human Resources and general office skills are further examples.

It is worth looking at the survey of skills at the beginning of section five. Relevant experience is the item most frequently demanded and that is primarily for management. At other levels, communication and administration skills are useful – all of which can be transferred. These skills are needed for jobs at a higher level which some will hope to attain. Others will find that these jobs are much less 'hands-on' and that they may not be as satisfying as the specialised job they first aspired to. Something to think about for the future is whether you aspire to senior management (very transferable) or want to stay much more 'hands-on'v.

SUGGESTION THREE – Political or Issue Commitment

I frequently give talks to final year students who are keen to get into development work. Sometimes I ask what they are interested in doing and often I hear answers such as Human Rights, then I discover that the individual has done nothing in the field. How will a future employer such as Amnesty International, for example, regard someone apparently 'keen to get into human rights' who has never written to a political prisoner, joined a demonstration, or become a member of a relevant organisation?

Sometimes the commitment can be as important as skills. In particular, in small and specialised agencies you have to be committed to the same cause, and very much on the same wavelength, to be able to share in the intense work of those engaged in advocacy or promotion of issues. You need to be able to share the gains and the disappointments as issues are debated at local, national or international level. This is most obvious in rights campaigns or in country-based issues, such as Tibet, Myanmar, etc.

My own example shows how a long-term political or issue commitment can have results. I returned from apartheid Namibia, then ruled by South Africa, changed by what I had witnessed. I stayed committed, joined a support group, wrote a regular newsletter and had a temporary one-year post helping Namibian students in the UK. Eight years later I got a desk officer job recruiting people to send to the wider southern African region. I had no personnel recruiting experience but my commitment got me the job. I learned on the job and have been recruiting ever since. The subsequent 22 years of commitment and experience has help to produce this book.

At a different level, John Manoochehri, a former policy adviser at the UN, suggests that national government decisions are important and need the right people:

> *"My opinion is that young professionals who want to participate in international debates should get experience in the international organisations as early as possible in their careers to broaden their vision and give them a picture of how complicated things can get! But after some meaningful experiencez... it might be more effective to work inside a national government: governments can and do override NGOs whenever they please, and it's a mistake to think that the UN system (or any Inter-Governmental Organisation with the possible exception of the World Trade Organisation) has much autonomous power at all".*[15]

See appendix A for a list of agencies with local groups that you could join, or BOND (British Overseas NGOs for Development; www.bond.org.uk) has a members list that will give you an idea of issue-based and country-specific NGOs.

SUGGESTION FOUR – Networking

> *"I was applying for lots of jobs and getting nowhere... Then a job as an environmental accountant came up... No less than five people sent me the advert, saying they thought it was the one for me. When I had the interview it turned out I had already met the interviewer in my networking – and I got the job".*[16]

Networking is useful for three reasons.

- First, many jobs are not advertised, either at all or only on agency, because of the high cost of media advertising. Some small NGOs prefer to work with people they know who share their commitment and will use known contacts. For these jobs you need to make yourself known to people who are looking for colleagues they feel they can

---

[15] Working in the United Nations; An insider's view on what's needed - on both sides. By John Manoochehri
[16] John Bent: The Alternative Careers Fair Handbook 2007. Oxford University

work with, so networking is essential. This is particularly true in small shared offices, where it is essential that staff get on well together and are equally committed to the same cause.

- Second, networking helps people within the sector to learn of other opportunities and of the realities of working within that particular organisation.

- Third, for those outside, it can answer some common questions, e.g. on the reputation of the NGO, the character of its managers, and whether its public statements reflect the reality of working within it.

Do you know someone with your skills who has worked or is working in development? How and where did they find their job? Can they suggest agencies or, better still, names of people to contact? Do you have family/friends or other contacts in UK or overseas charities or NGOs? If so, can they provide you with helpful leads?

Some other ideas:

- use your contacts or create them by attending conferences, workshops, seminars or even rallies and demonstrations. Show you are committed;

- talk to the stallholders at careers fairs and other people working in the sector. Ask how they got into their work, and who you should talk to;

- approach speakers at conferences. Telephone or email people once you have their permission. Ask if you can contact them for some advice. Tell these people briefly what you are interested in. Don't ask how you might get to do their job, but how you could get your foot on the ladder, e.g. do they know of ways in? Always thank those who have helped you by email or letter. They might remember you when a job comes up;

- know what you can offer and what your particular interests are, without being too self limiting, in case the conversation goes further;

- use contacts from your academic past – alumni who may have worked their way up.

- join a professional association in your relevant field;

- more up-front tactics include walking into big NGOs and asking about vacancies or to meet the Human Resources staff; sending off speculative letters and following this up with a phone call and even advertising yourself in the local press or professional magazines. Some of these tactics may apply in the commercial sector where self-promotion might indicate that you could also sell goods or services although most HR staff prefer not to have to deal with cold-callers and speculative applications. You have nothing to lose by trying this tactic; if you do nothing, then you'll gain nothing!

SUGGESTION FIVE – Volunteering

Many talented and qualified people work for no pay simply because they want to join a particular interest group and/or respond to the demands of their conscience. Both those reasons are highly commendable but volunteering can also help with future employment.

"*Two thirds of employers... would choose to employ someone with volunteer experience*".[17]

Experience of working or studying away from home in a different environment or culture, whether in the UK or overseas, (but preferably in a developing country, rather than in Western Europe, North America or Australasia), can be important in providing proof in several areas that NGOs look for, survivability, health and commitment among them. It is also important in some work areas such as counselling, social work, etc., where experience is often needed to be able to get onto the course or as part of the training. If work experience is a necessary part of a qualification, then course organisers will normally have their own contacts. However, if they leave it to you, or you want to test out a new career possibility, then try www.work-experience.org, www.greenforce. org for environmental placements and IAESTE (international placements especially for IT, engineering and science students; www.iaeste.org.uk). For tailor-made opportunities for more skilled volunteers, try the specialist site, www.2way.org.uk. In other areas such as advocacy, volunteering can be significant in making contacts and learning about possible jobs (Networking, suggestion 4).

The networks you establish may produce a job. You can ask for permission to sit in on conference discussions or other networking possibilities. Another site (Edinburgh University) www.careers.ed.ac.uk emphasises the benefits of networking as: learning new skills, experience, meeting new people, giving something back, learning more about a cause, improving confidence and feeling of self-worth.

East Anglia University site, www.uea.ac.uk/careers, warns that volunteers may be asked to do relatively menial tasks, but enthusiasm will hopefully impress people who may, at the very least, be useful referees. If you feel exploited - some say they only get mundane tasks such as envelope-stuffing – ask for more variety of work or how you can learn more about the work of the organisation. If you are not satisfied that your tasks are equal to those promised, then leave and find an alternative placement.

In the UK

- Start with your local volunteer bureau which you can find on www.volunteering.org.uk or look for opportunities on www.timebank.org.uk; even a few hours a week helps. A growing number of UK cities have a local version of the site www.gumtree.com, another place to look.

- Frequently national groups get concessions to advertise in the press. Look in the Wednesday edition of *The Guardian* at their occasional volunteer feature, the Monday edition of the *London Evening Standard* and the *Big Issue*.

- UK volunteer opportunities can be found through www.do-it.org.uk and www. evolunteer.co.uk.

- If you have a particular interest in community work try Community Service Volunteers (www.csv.org.uk), This organisation gives a small weekly allowance and provides free accommodation for residential volunteers. If your interest is in conservation, try British Trust for Conservation Volunteers (www.btcv.org.uk).

---

[17] Croner: Management of Voluntary Organisations Newsletter. www.croner.co.uk

- See also the list at Appendix A of national organisations with local groups.

- Virtual volunteering is becoming more popular and allows you to work at your own time and remotely from the organisation. Virtual opportunities can be found by searching the Internet and on www.timebank.org.uk and www.volunteermatch.org.

- For summer breaks in the UK or overseas, see www.vacationwork.co.uk. However, if you have a career in mind and are using this to gain experience and show commitment, avoid 'adventure-based' volunteering, which is less valued by employers unless you can show some other real involvement in development.

- If you have skills from your previous work, you could try REACH at www.volwork.org.uk. If you have IT skills you could offer these through www.unv.org.

- Mature people could look at possibilities in the publication, *Gap Years for Grown Ups* by Susan Griffith[18] or www.gapyearforgrownups.co.uk.

- Many charities need trustees, people to advise on management, finance, personnel or with expertise in its work.

Overseas

The best source of information on 300+ agencies is the sister book to this one, the *Guide to Volunteering for Development* (see www.wse.org.uk).

- Search by place and time on www.wwv.org.uk and www.springboard.hobsons.co.uk. In popular places, the choice will be enormous, in others perhaps none at all. There may be a fee.

- Christians Abroad gives advice on possibilities for Christian volunteers, as well as its own opportunities – www.cabroad.org.uk.

- On www.howtobooks.co.uk, you will find details of several specialist areas, including *Green Volunteers*.

- BOND lists unpaid vacancies under 'jobs' on www.bond.org.uk.

- www.avso.org is an EU sponsored volunteering association for the EU and beyond.

- Though Canadian-based, www.awid.org has many links to development organisations and is especially strong on women's rights.

- In Ireland, Comhlamh (www.comhlamh.org) gives helpful advice, and publishes a directory of opportunities with Irish development agencies. www.workwithus.org is similar for Scotland, but also includes jobs.

- You can simply go and find what is available wherever you are. Some predeparture research will help; www.devdir.org and www.serveyourworld.com give details of NGOs across the world. Among the most popular countries are South Africa (NGO list at www.sangonet.org.za; and also visit www.volunteer.co.za) and India (see www.indiafocus.indiainfo.com). Nigerian NGOs are on www.nnngo.org. If you want to know more about other country NGOs then look at www.wango.org.

- www.charityjob.co.uk is a job site but around one third of its vacancies are voluntary.

---

[18] Vacation Work Publications

Why not test it out through the programme *Development from the Inside*, that gives a four week introduction in India, including seminars with local activists and a placement in a local project; see links via www.charitiesadvisorytrust.co.uk.

Maybe you don't want to volunteer in the developing world but would like to do some short-term work somewhere else in return for food and accommodation. If so, you will find a range of opportunities for manual work at www.workaway.info.

Further notes:

■ Adventure trips may provide some team building opportunities as well as fun, but they may not give much contact with local people. Sometimes such trips are called 'mobile ghettos' meaning they only have a small 'development' content. For that reason they are often not regarded as highly in the sector as other forms of overseas volunteering.

■ Despite its name, VSO (Voluntary Service Overseas) isn't for volunteers in the usual sense but requires a relevant qualification and at least two years work experience. VSO offer good UK support and local overseas salaries for two year appointments; www.vso.org.uk.

■ Travel responsibly and check the following for both volunteering sites and ethical business links, www.tourismconcern.org.uk, which also publishes the *Good Alternative Travel Guide* by Mark Man.

■ Whatever you try, you have to make your own judgement about the agency or opportunity once you come across it.

How do you choose a volunteer placement?

■ Follow up personal recommendations.

■ Ask the organisation to put you in touch with returned volunteers.

■ Check the website, not just the aims and objectives, but what has really been achieved and what your contribution might be.

■ Is the organisation a registered charity, not for profit or only a company? UK-based charities can be checked out via the Charity Commission www.charity-commission.gov.uk. A website ending .org is normally a charity, short for organisation: i.e. not for profit. Originally designated for not for profit firms and any other organisations that did not fit under the .com or .net extension, any individual or business may register a .org domain name.[19]

■ NCVO (National Council for Voluntary Organisations) can verify UK-based agencies.

■ Check the terms and conditions to see what are you committing yourself too; how much free time there is; are there other volunteers; what are living conditions like; how urban or remote is the placement? etc.

■ Is there a fee? If so, does it go to the project or does it stay in the UK? What do you get for the fee? Is it preparation, support, de-briefing?

■ Calculate the cost and do your sums. For overseas placements you will almost certainly have to pay for the flight and pre-departure vaccinations, etc. You will also need travel insurance (try www.wse.org.uk for this), visas or work permits, accommodation and living expenses. Some placements within the UK such as in community work will provide accommodation and some living costs.

■ Once you are there, do you want to do some additional travel to other parts of the region or country? Is this permitted? Will your insurance cover it? Will your visa permit re-entry?

■ For travel information on individual countries, check out www.fco.gov.uk, for Government advice and a helpful 'Know before you Go' section.

■ Remember that your travel insurance may not cover situations where your government advises against travel or where your placement includes manual work. For the latter, World Service Enquiry (www.wse.org.uk) can arrange insurance.

SUGGESTION SIX – Internships and Academic High Flyers

Internships

Internships can provide a good way into development work, but it is a very competitive field. Be careful, as many advertised 'internships' or 'graduate programmes' (especially in the USA) are in effect unpaid volunteer schemes; some may even require you to pay. Also check whether they provide genuine training or any networking possibilities.

There may be a chance of a future job with the same organisation, although some, such as the World Bank, prohibit this for a period. However, gaining experience and proving yourself should be the main purpose. Some are based in large international or government bodies, but these are usually very competitive. Most university careers offices will have lists of internships known to them that may be linked to their courses or international connections.

Internationally, a good place to start is www.idealist.org. You can search by country or key word(s).

■ For current possibilities look at www.experiencedevelopment.org. In one month these possibilities included ACTSA (Action for Southern Africa), Alliances for Africa, Centre for Democracy and Development, Christian Aid, Human Rights Watch, Intermediate Technology Group, International Alert, RefAid and the World Bank.

■ Many universities' career services offer information about ways into development and details of internships. For example, CEDC at The University of Sussex has useful advice and many links; www.sussex.ac.uk/cdec.

■ To get into the UN as well as building up specific expertise, there is another way: "*The second option is to get an internship, and try to develop something on the basis of the connections and experience that gives you. Lots of people move smoothly from internships to consultancies, a reputable platform from which to develop career options both inside and outside the UN/IGO system*". The United Nations has a self-funded internship scheme, www.unv.org or you can offer online volunteering help.

- Medical students or those enrolled on related courses (including engineering and administration as well as public health) can be taken on by the International Medical Corps. They have paid and unpaid internships and transport, insurance, accommodation and food is provided. www.imcworldwide.org.

- The UNHCR (UN High Commission for Refugees) has unpaid internships in London.

- The Organisation for Economic Cooperation and Development (OECD; www.oecd.org) has a similar scheme to the World Bank. Vacancies are advertised in the 2nd half of the year for programmes starting one year later. OECD also has a Trainee scheme, advertised for a few weeks at the beginning of each year – www.oecd.org

- The Overseas Development Institute (ODI; www.odi.org.uk/fellows/index.html) has a Fellowship Scheme, sending young postgraduates on two-year assignments to work in the public sectors of developing countries. Recruitment begins each October.

- The Foreign Policy Centre (www.fpc.org.uk) offers expenses-paid internships for up to six months.

- Student Force (www.studentforce.org.uk) is a national charity focusing on environmental issues that helps people boost their employability. Also try www.peopleandplanet.org.uk.

- British MPs often have opportunities for recent graduates or students as researchers, but check whether this is relevant to your career goals. Contact your MP to see what might be possible; party allegiance is usually irrelevant.

- Christian Aid (www.christian-aid.org.uk) has a paid Internship Scheme, mostly London office based. For people aged 18-25, they have a Gap Year Scheme, based in UK area offices with a two-week overseas trip funded by Christian Aid.

- The National Graduate Training Programme (www.ngdp.co.uk) gives placements with UK local authorities which can be useful experience.

- The majority of internships are USA-based and most provide little or no remuneration. Further details can be found on the internet; simply type 'internship' into Goggle.

- The Erasmus programme of the EU (www.esn.org) gives funded assistance for students to study and gain related work experience throughout Europe.

- www.crossculturalsolutions.org has an internship programme which is similar to its volunteer programme but with academic targets.

- The Charities Advisory Trust has paid internships for staff in its pre-Christmas card shops and its *Good Gifts* Catalogue Programme.

- A good place to find a summary of many of these is www.waterberry.org. Look at their young professionals programs as well as internships.

Academic High Flyers

There are limited possibilities for those who do exceptionally well academically to go straight onto government or internationally-sponsored jobs. These are internships with a bit more clout, and often have a high training element. Survival and promotion may depend on performance, as in commercial parallels. Some of these schemes may be advertised as internships but others will use different terminology.

For many, the ultimate goal is a United Nations job, but their main scheme is self-funded (www.unv.org). The UK government has a 'Fast Stream' programme (not just in development) that requires a post graduate qualification in a specialism, 12 months experience first in a developing country or in development work. This leads to a five-year (maximum) training programme within DFID and can then lead to high level posts; www.faststream.gov.uk.

The World Bank (www.worldbank.org) has a Young Professionals Scheme, asking for high professional achievement as well as leadership potential, as does the OECD, but each of these is heavily over-subscribed. Beware too that sometimes an organisation like the World Bank will not allow you to proceed into employment within the same organisation.

SUGGESTION SEVEN – Non-Development Charity Work

According to the NCVO (National Council for Voluntary Organisations; www.ncvo-vol.org.uk) there are 169,000 general charities in the UK employing 608,000 people (231,000 part-time). There are clearly many overlaps and common concerns with NGOs that are not directly involved in world development. Many cover issues of common interest in both 'developing' and 'developed' countries such as Human Rights, Health, Education, Fair Trade. The two most requested areas are Health and Education and these are the easiest ways to transfer to direct work in the sector. All the administrative, fundraising, management, advocacy and promotion skills (among others) are clearly transferable too. It is still important to show your commitment to development tasks through membership and volunteering, just as in any job in this sector. It is also an area in which networking is helpful as most umbrella groups and training events will cover a wide scope of NGOs and will give opportunities to network with those concentrating on Development.

Working for a Charity (www.wfac.org.uk) provides information about working in the voluntary sector and specialist training courses that offer information and advice to career changers, returnees to work and new graduates on how to transfer their skills effectively into the sector and the challenges and management issues they will face.

The best sites for general jobs are www.charityjob.co.uk, www.charitypeople.co.uk and http://nfpjobs.netxtra.net. You could look for listings of specialist recruiting agencies on www.charityconnections.co.uk and www.volresources.org.uk. The Wednesday edition of *The Guardian* is the best national newspaper source of jobs; http://jobs.guardian.co.uk. Charity People also organise the only voluntary sector fair, Forum3 (www.forum3.co.uk), each October.

SUGGESTION EIGHT – Teaching English Overseas

There are many openings for TEFL (Teachers of English as a Foreign Language) or TESOL (Teaching English to Speakers of Other Languages), particularly in Eastern Europe and Asia specifically China, Korea and Japan. In this sector there are clear divisions between short-term volunteers (who can make a contribution to the learning of English) and those who are professionally qualified. For volunteers it is one of the commonest jobs, but it can't become a career or make a substantial impact on Development without relevant training and this does not include the weekend TEFL courses offered by some volunteer-sending agencies. The minimum level is a one-month Certificate. Native English speakers are best placed to get jobs as Teachers of English as a Foreign/Second Language without experience or qualifications, but increasingly employers and overseas governments require teachers with a TEFL/TESOL qualification plus experience, in addition to a first degree. Many even insist on an MA Linguistics/TEFL/TESOL postgraduate qualification. The most highly paid jobs in EFL often require a one-year TEFL Diploma and considerable experience. If TEFL work is simply a passport to travel, a one-month intensive training course would probably be enough. It is advisable to do a course which is externally recognised and offers classroom experience. The British Council (www.britishcouncil.org) produces information about courses, study centres and much more.

A few requests come from developing countries for qualified and experienced graduate teachers of EFL, although the demand for Secondary teachers of English is considerably greater. High levels of English are needed for tertiary education in many former British colonies.

CELTA (Certificate in English Language Teaching to Adults, formerly the RSA/Cambridge Certificate), or the Trinity College TESOL Certificate are the most acceptable qualifications to employers. CELTA is the best known and most widely taken initial TESOL/TEFL qualification. Details for ESOL University of Cambridge can be found at www.cambridgeesol.org.

Distance learning can be done through the Internet. www.tefl.com, www.teflonline.net, www.englishtc.co.uk and www.europa-pages.com are good places to start if you are looking for courses and more information. Look for courses' that have The Accreditation Council for TESOL Distance Education Courses stamp of approval. There are a great many TEFL course providers. The level of the course you decide to take will depend upon your career goal. It is advisable to research as much as possible before paying for a course.

A good source for both long- and short-term vacancies can be found on www.tefl.com.

SUGGESTION NINE – Joining In

Joining local, national or international charities or NGOs is another way of showing your commitment, and is vital in any NGO interview, especially for work in campaigning and advocacy. It can also give useful contacts, and access to the house literature and that of other NGOs where jobs are often advertised much more cheaply than in the national press.

Would you be taken seriously by a peace campaigning group if you had never marched for peace? How can you show your environmental interest if you have not joined Friends of the Earth (or similar), or concern for the homeless if you have not supported Shelter or bought the Big Issue? An interest isn't enough!

Local volunteer groups can be a good start but local offices of national organisations will be best for networking. See Appendix B for more details.

SUGGESTION TEN – Temping

Temporary work is a way of getting to know how organisations work, what they are looking for, and what you enjoy. It is not always secretarial although those skills are immensely useful now at senior level in all organisations. If you are pro-active it can be a way of showing a potential employer how good you are (and without being exploited, which is one issue sometimes perceived in volunteering), you could show what you can do over and above the actual job. You may find it difficult to link only to NGOs in this way, but the practical experience is what counts.

Be careful though as some temping agencies have deals that penalise organisations that then decide to take on any temps placed with them. For more see http://jobsadvice.guardian.co.uk. However, all this will only be true in larger NGOs. Smaller NGOs will have more opportunities for volunteering.

> *"I did a lot of temporary office work which, while often boring, actually provided me with a lot of experience of how offices work and developed my IT skills, which have proven to be indispensable to my current job."*[20]

Temporary jobs are listed on www.charitypeople.co.uk. In the FAQ section of their website they state "If there is a specific charity or specific type of charity you wish to work for, temping is an excellent way to get your foot in the door".

These are not the only ways; some other ideas could be…

Oxford University runs an Alternative Careers Fair (as many other universities do) and part of their advice is to suggest that alternatives include working within the UK scene. The options require the same motivation and commitment and have equal importance in changing people's lives and futures. They are good ways to demonstrate commitment and skills. They suggest you could:

- Teach in an inner-city school;

- Work in a government department;

- Campaign or work for a pressure group campaigning for more equitable wealth distribution;

- Train as a social worker;

- Volunteer on a city farm;

- Become a host family providing holidays for children from deprived areas;

- Work for a charity, raising funds;

- Donate a percentage of income to charities;

- Become an Member of Parliament!

Now you know some ways in, what jobs there are and something about yourself and the sector, let's next look at the skills you need; and how can you develop them?

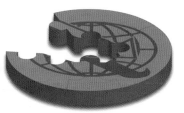

SECTION FIVE:
Skills

What Skills Are Needed?

A period of volunteering will prove both your commitment and your ability to survive physically and cross-culturally; two of the three vital areas listed in section two. Now, it depends on your skills and on how you present yourself.

Within development jobs, the skills most requested relate to five broad areas. These are:

- Advisory: Business experts, economists, agronomists and academics. These can be short-term contracts or consultancy roles;

- Teaching: This is the expertise requested most by the UK's largest sending agency, VSO. The need to learn English for international communication or higher education means that English teaching will remain a major work opportunity for the foreseeable future. However, there are also examples of volunteers being exploited by less than professional 'schools' and some work concentrates on the business world or those able to pay fees. A TEFL Certificate level qualification is usually required;

- Health professionals: this expertise is required partly to compensate for the huge numbers from developing countries attracted to work in the developed world, and training roles can be important. Tropical health qualifications and/or training are obviously useful assets;

- Technical: Sanitation engineers, logistics and finance experts. This is a growing area and can be short-term, especially when dealing with response to disasters. Training roles can be important here too;

- Management and project administrators: This area is less specialised in one sense, and often more generalist (such as managers, executives, planners) but is the area in which most vacancies will be found in our *Opportunities Abroad*. Within this last group, 'Project Manager' or 'Country coordinator' are the most desired roles since they mean you are in charge, responsible for making changes, achieving measurable results and making a difference to people's lives which is the fundamental reason for involvement in development work.

---

[21] More in formation from www.sussex.ac.uk/cdec

Within this range of jobs there are different requirements on the skills front. Some need a wide variety but others need specific regional and specialist expertise. Interestingly, an analysis of skills listed in advertisements for high-level jobs showed a significant difference between those at that level and the next level down.

No-one will get to the higher level kind of job immediately, but it might be worth considering possible routes if you are the kind of person who desires to be at the top. It is a common aim to want to manage and control but you need to think whether you might be happier doing something else. As you go further into management and control, there is usually less face-to-face contact with the people you are aiming to help. Is that what you want?

Top level jobs

Significantly, and perhaps obviously, the top-level jobs want experience in both the realities of the sector and in managing both people and money. In twelve advertised jobs for programme manager or similar the following skills were identified:

- relevant experience (10) – this might be either in one of the areas listed next or in a region of the world;

- experience in programme management (9) and in staff management (8);

- relating to other NGOs or donors such as government or international funders (7) and interpersonal skills (6) were the next highest single items.

In addition there were the following: communication, development awareness, financial accountability (5 each), masters degree, local language, proposal writing, and ability to work under pressure or in an insecure environment (4 each), analytical skills, computer skills, monitoring or research experience, partner relationship building and regional knowledge (3 each).

These are clearly jobs to which most people could only progress after some years, and it is significant that the highest scoring skills are quite generalist. Local language knowledge scores only 4, suggesting that top-level negotiations are in English. Significantly, USA-based agencies seem to ask for less in language skills. Moreover, the list mostly consists of transferable skills – once you've done it in one place you can do it in another.

A typical overseas job at this level would be a Country Director. One such job had the following list of 'essential duties and responsibilities':

- recruit, hire, manage and lead staff, consultants and contractors to ensure efficient and timely implementation of project activities;

- provide overall policy guidance, training and leadership to all staff members;

- conduct routine project needs assessments and programme reviews to ensure successful implementation and donor compliance;

- ensure the timeliness, cost and quality of all activities performed;

- coordinate, oversee and ensure the quality of all training activities under the grant;

- liaise with donors at UN, home government and international agency level, and regional and central authorities, other development organisations involved in similar assistance programmes in the region and local communities to ensure support, coordination and satisfaction;

- prepare a monthly report to the HQ;

- prepare quarterly and/or semi annual reports according to donor requirements;

- aggressively and proactively identify new programme opportunities and provide regular updates and recommendations to the HQ;

- develop new programmes for additional funding in existing programmes and for new projects in country;

- prepare annual work plan and budget that identifies key objectives, responsible staff, desirables and potential roadblocks.

Personal requirements were of 10 years experience implementing development programmes with 5 years at senior level. Only later in 'Education and/or Experience Requirements', does the advertisement identify a country, but requests only *"knowledge of the issues related to project feasibility in the assigned region"*. In other words, experience in similar situations is acceptable and detailed knowledge of the location is not essential. Transfer of skills is far more important.

Second level jobs

At the next level down (from 15 jobs analysed) the highest skills were:

- communication (9)
- second language (8)
- administration (7)
- monitoring or research, a special academic knowledge, and adaptability (6 each) were next.

Also mentioned were:

- need for mobility/frequent travel;
- creativity;
- ability to inspire;
- programme design;
- ability to relate to people at all levels;
- resourcefulness;
- analytical skills;
- willingness to learn;
- ability to work under pressure.

People from the UK are not known for their language skills (the second highest score above), but another language is a great asset. The most common and therefore most useful languages to know are English, French, Spanish and Arabic. Some jobs require fluency, both oral and written, in the national language or occasionally the local language or dialect. Sometimes agencies may consider applicants for a job with a prerequisite language if the applicant has proven ability to learn another language. Unless you are a TEFL or language teacher or hope to act as a translator, language alone is not a sufficient skill to qualify you for an overseas job. Translators are often recruited locally or will be native-speakers who also know the language of the sending/funding agency.

A second level job is more specific and practical, less policy or management-based, especially in larger organisations, and often requires close working with colleagues. So staff management scores only 4, equal to team player and cultural sensitivity. Scores for adaptability (6), self-motivation (5) and capacity building (5, but 0 in top jobs) are higher at this level, as are regional knowledge, local experience and specialist capabilities – all vital in building relationships at co-worker and local agency level. A good top manager can, on this theory, manage anywhere.

Another analysis of a different month might produce different detailed figures but the general message is the same: specific skills practised and proven at local level with the flexibility and adaptability required for these jobs will prove your worth, and from that experience it should be possible to move to the more generalist senior jobs in which management of people, programmes and finance are all important. Specialist skills are still important, whether in engineering, medicine or other areas, but more time will be spent in those general activities, in policy-making and negotiation with government and other bodies.

Clearly there are overlaps and different recruiters use words in different ways, but the above analysis gives an idea of the kind of skills that are required in addition to any specific job related ones or qualifications in accountancy, law, health, engineering, etc. Academic qualifications may be one required proof of skill or knowledge and this is increasingly being requested for work permits. For example, recently recruited teachers for Tanzania had to show that the content of their own academic course was directly relevant to their job – so to teach history, a course in African history was needed to get the work permit.

At this level there are overseas jobs supervised by Country Directors (such as in the example above). These will often require much more specific skills, and although there will always be a level of reporting, this will usually be to the Country Director and not to HQ. A job for a Water/Sanitation Engineer, for example, had the following:

Assessment of emergency situations and drafting concept papers in response to the crises assessed, detailing immediate water and sanitation rehabilitation needs, water development, water distribution, storage, chlorination/filtration and human waste management.

In detail:

- plan daily activities for water and sanitation programme;
- carry out water quality analysis and train local staff in water quality monitoring;
- design and construction of water distribution network and storage;
- supervise logistics and procurement of all necessary items and materials for projects;
- design and implement activities for latrine constructions;

- write proposals and plans for water and sanitation intervention;
- compile monthly reports, programme/project documents and budgets;
- training and building local capacity in production and maintenance of water and sanitation projects.

Unlike the Country Director job, this job required a specific bachelor's degree (in water/sanitation/public health areas), plus 5 years relevant work experience, of which 3 should be in a development programme.

Simona Santojanni, Development Officer for Lawyers for Liberty wrote:

"With no proper work experience in the field I erroneously thought there was no chance of finding a job within this fascinating sector, but I couldn't be more wrong. The experience gained in other business, my voluntary work during university and a genuine interest in the subject all played an important role when I started to look for a job in a Human Rights o rganisation".[22]

First level

A listing of jobs from VSO for returned volunteers in February 2007 included the following:

Overseas	UK based
Electrical Engineer	Education Adviser
Land Surveyor	Marketing Analyst
Business Development Adviser	Fundraiser
Construction Work Teacher	Account Manager
Vehicle Engineer	Public Policy Adviser
Programme Manager	Campaigns Manager on Climate Change
HIV/AIDS Programme Coordinator	Volunteer Development Officer
Science Teacher	Events Coordinator
TEFL Teacher	Teacher
School Matron	Accountant

They also listed agencies interested in speculative applications as varied as Recycle (the bike charity, that ships repaired cycles overseas) to The Halo Trust (landmine clearance), Peaceworkers UK (Human Rights monitors) and Concern Worldwide (Country management, Accountants, etc.).

---

[22] www.careers.ox.ac.uk/documents/alternative_careers_fair_2007_handbook.pdf

Typical of these is their relative specialism, though the job may include a variety of other tasks. This sounds odd, but the reality is that while the specialism is advertised, the job will need other skills because there will possibly be few colleagues. In the Halo Trust example there are 7,000 national staff and 30 expatriates. The expatriates, the majority of whom join in their late 20s or 30s, will bring additional skills such as IT, management or bookkeeping which may not be available locally.V The jobs may be wider than thought, and this will help the moving on process, particularly in small NGOs. These are ideal jobs for those who have some experience and/or are keen to use practical skills and be involved at grass-roots level.

This is the level at which most people enter the development sector, all except those with more transferable expertise or high level management experience. The question is: if you are moving into development, how do you show that your skills are adequate and how do you develop those you need? Even to get that first level job, what do you need to get there? It's increasingly difficult (if not impossible) to get into the development sector at first-level in an overseas based role, although much easier in a UK-based role where administrative and other jobs have to be filled. These entry-level jobs are in a whole variety of areas and no different from the rest of the job market in many respects. It is easier to transfer from a parallel job with a few years experience (e.g. in accounting or teaching) and the advice in Section four should give some ideas of how to make the initial move. However, for any job it is important to be able to present yourself as a skilled individual. It is simple to find out the skills most frequently asked for (as in the survey above) but to do that self-presentation, you need to know what skills you have. Reading the following section may reveal skills you did not know about or realise were important, including soft skills. Hopefully it will give you confidence to make the move.

Skill Types

Charity People (www.charitypeople.com) suggest in their article 'First Job in a Charity' that you should think of your skills in three ways. Skills need to be:

- Relevant

- Measurable

- Realistic

This is common sense. Skills need to relate to the job and you need to be able to prove their quality against criteria or competence tables in particular professions.

The abilities you have – your skills – are seen by others in both the things you have already done and the person you are. The first can be harder to prove for recent graduates, but not out of the question; see "soft skills" below. The second will help you to match person specifications which are part of some job descriptions, but these personal qualities have to be proven just as much as showing the things you have done. How do you 'measure' against the skills asked for and how has your performance been 'measured'? If, for example, you describe yourself as 'adaptable' what does that mean and can you give an example? (See also CV advice).

Hard and soft skills

Skills can be grouped into two groups – hard and soft. Hard skills are those you need to match the job description (accountant, engineer, etc) and demonstrate experience or qualification in a specified area. Hard skills are what you can do, soft skills can be the result of experience (often through training others etc.) and can be learned, but are usually more related to your personality or natural traits. Two people with identical qualifications, experience and training (hard skills) may be observed as very different team leaders. Reliability, responsibility, creativity, compassion, are all soft skills, and it is often these that will push you above others in any short-listing, particularly at interview, and make you effective in the job. Soft skills have been described as a "function of personality characteristics" and will include motivation, work ethic and interpersonal ability.

Don't ignore your soft skills, often produced by part-time, voluntary or community work. Ask yourself what information/data work, people skills, practical activities and ideas you have developed. As a waitress/waiter you might develop skills in negotiation, listening, quick thinking or handling pressure. As a community worker you might develop greater tolerance, organisation, fundraising, listening skills, become cross-culturally considerate and understanding, and perhaps also competent to negotiate with local authorities.

Recognise your aptitude and natural skills. Most of us can do something well without any thought or effort while others would struggle and most people do not recognise or rate their natural abilities or work out the skills they have. What comes easily to you? What natural soft or hard skills do you have?

Practical skills

Practical skills can be obvious such as carpentry, building, language, IT, etc., while others are often hidden and not recognised by the holder. Not everyone can run an office, repair a car, manage a website, do the odd bit of accounting and write good publicity leaflets, but these might be useful where the staff is small or less well-trained (overseas jobs included). It is worth looking also at what academic studies are needed. For example, someone with a history degree may not use their 'knowledge' but could emphasise research and presentation skills and background knowledge on issues as wide as colonial history and cultural identity. A maths graduate could emphasise accuracy, logic and the determination to achieve results.

Transferable skills

"Most positions in the not-for-profit sector require skills that are directly transferable from the private sector. You need to be able to sell these transferable skills relevant to the types of positions you are interested in." [23]

Transferable skills are crucial, especially as people frequently move in and out of the sector. Obvious ones are where particular specialisms are required as in medicine. However they can be equally important in administration, office management, human resources, finance, IT, public relations, communications or sales, which is, for example,

---

[23] Charity People's FAQ section on their website www.charitypeople.co.uk

transferable to fundraising. It is the skills you use within the roles and not the work itself that is relevant.

There is a large amount of research in the area of transferable skills and numerous reports from universities and commercial sources. A study by of employer ratings of 15 personal transferable skills by Exeter University put effective communication, team work, ability to solve problems, analytical skills, flexibility and adaptability at the top. At the bottom were IT, relating to wider context and specialist subject knowledge, all of which suggests that people skills are more important than detailed knowledge (particularly at graduate level).

Quintessential Careers has a lot of information on this at www.quintcareers.com and suggests transferable skills can be grouped as:

- communication;
- research and planning;
- human relations;
- organisational management and leadership;
- work survival.

There are around 12 sub-headings in each category. For example, within 'work survival' are: cooperation, enforcing policies, punctuality, time management, attention to detail, meeting goals, enlisting help, accepting responsibility, setting and meeting deadlines, organising, making and implementing decisions. Other groupings may call many of these 'people skills'. The general list of around 60 items could be useful in CV writing but don't choose too many or those not relevant to the job description.

Discover Your Skills

There are many ways to assess your skills, and you could start with the list in Section six that will help you to fine-tune your CV. Once the gaps have been identified it would be worth thinking through how many would be useful in a work situation. For those at university, you will find that the careers service has its own tests and lists, and for others there are plenty of possibilities.

- Skills assessment can be done online, mostly through US sites so allowances need to be made for differences in culture and language. www.assessment.com is one site, giving a multiple-choice questionnaire of most/least likely in 71 different areas. You can get a print out giving suggestions on possible occupation areas. For full detailed information there is a charge.

- The Occupational Information Network (http://online.onetcenter.org) provides a similar resource with a shorter questionnaire in which you identify your skills within their categories: basic, social, complex problem solving, technical, systems and resource management. It will also give you a summary of skills required for certain jobs

- One UK based site is http://uk.tickle.com that has a charge. www.prospects.ac.uk is particularly useful for under and recent graduates.

- Part of the Windmills Programme looks at skills, particularly in relation to CV writing, helping you to match them to advertised jobs, www.windmillsonline.co.uk, www. jobhuntersbible.com offers an assessment of the programmes offered by other sites.

- Some employers use psychometric tests to gauge aptitude and personality, and information on some of these can be found on www.psychorpcenter.com and http:// doctorjob.com/testingzone.

The Windmills Programme suggests grouping your skills under four skill headings: self-reliance, people, specialist and general. Map skills from positive parts of your career; including activities outside normal work; putting yourself in the shoes of three people who know you well, such as friends or colleagues, for what you believe they would say about you. You could even ask them before making a final revision.

If you do all of this, the result of all this will be a your 'Skills Portfolio' which can be drawn upon to write applications letters, edit your CV or simply to measure yourself against requested people skills. Most jobs want both specialist skills and more general people ones, and sometimes a skill can be transferred from one sector to another. Specific language skills might be a requirement for a job concerned with a region of the world, but for another job they might prove you could learn other languages, or simply that you could relate better cross-culturally. There is more on this in Improving your CV (page 68) and application procedures, including a suggestion of active words useful to describe your skills.

Develop Your Skills

Training and courses

While there are jobs for which training is essential or legally necessary before you start, whether in health work, counselling, as an electrician or in the police service, for most areas there is nothing to beat the value of experience. Where specific skills are required, it will also help to have attended relevant recent training courses, but only after doing something that shows you have qualifications, proven skills and experience in a wider area of your specialism. So, for management, you need to show that you have managed people and money, for human rights work, a basic knowledge and practice of law will help. You might then train for a more specialised area and then be able to apply for advertised jobs.

An example: RedR (www.redr.org.uk) run an annual course, 'Water Supply, Treatment and Distribution in Emergencies', work which is of crucial significance after a major disaster, when safe, clean water is vital for survival. The course states that it is intended for those who already manage water supply projects and *professionals who wish to adapt their skills to humanitarian work in this subject*".

Specialist courses are not cheap; the three-day RedR course quoted above costs between £350 and £490. It is not advisable to attend training for something not within your skill area or which you feel will simply help you 'get into development'.

Many small development NGOs can't afford training packages for their own staff and this is one of the reasons that people are increasingly moving in and out of the sector:

"Training by development organisations themselves is rare". [24]

Some academic centres and NGOs provide specialist short courses which, depending on your specialism, may be helpful. Information about short courses can be obtained from BOND (British NGOs for Development) on www.bond.org.uk and Bioforce (www. bioforce.asso.fr). Medair (www.medair.org) run a 10 day orientation training on relief and rehabilitation. RedR (www.redr.org.uk) run courses in many centres around the world.

Also look at:

- Development Training and Learning Programme http://www.dtalk.ie;
- Expedition Medicine & Leadership www.expeditionmedicine.co.uk;
- London School of Hygiene & Tropical Medicine www.lshtm.ac.uk;
- Merlin www.merlin.org.uk;
- PeaceworkersUK www.peaceworkers.org.uk;
- Responding to Conflict www.respond.org.

Reliefweb (www.reliefweb.int) also lists organisations offering training. Your career goal may help you decide what to study and at what level. You may find it helpful to seek advice on the relevance of study from an organisations Human Resource department or someone working in a similar field. We can advise you in a *One to One* or you may find *e>volve*, our unique email self-coaching service helpful. Details can be found on our site at www.wse.org.uk.

In the wider voluntary sector there are many training possibilities for people who want to increase their chances by improving marketable workplace skills.

- The Directory of Social Change offer courses from fund-raising to writing effective promotional material, effective administration, training and presentation skills: www. dsc.org.uk
- The Centre for Strategy and Communication offer similar courses: www.the-centre.co.uk.
- INTRAC (The International NGO Training and Research Centre) www.intrac.org has a wide variety of courses.
- Other management courses for the sector, usually at a higher level, can be found on www.evaluation.org.uk. A free handbook on self-evaluation, *How well are we doing?* is also available from this source.
- The Institute of Cultural Affairs runs training courses linked to its volunteer programme: www.ica-uk.org.uk.
- The Projects Company runs short courses on project management, fundraising, etc.: www.theprojectsco.co.uk.
- The Charities Advisory Trust has a month-long training course based in India entitled *'Development from the inside'*: www.charitiesadvisorytrust.org.uk.
- If you are based in the Republic of Ireland try www.comhlamh.org.

Distance-learning courses in management of the Voluntary Sector are possible through

The Open University Business School (www.open.ac.uk/oubs) and at The University of Wales at Lampeter (www.lamp.ac.uk).

Development Degree

Additional academic training can be beneficial personally and professionally. However, for most people it is more important to make further academic study relevant to existing qualifications or work. An Engineer, Doctor, Social Worker or Accountant might specialise in something relevant to development work and this would be more helpful than a degree in Development Studies.

So how would a development degree itself help? Teachers of Development, including those in local Development Studies Centres, will clearly need higher academic qualifications than those being taught. A Master's degree is the minimum for university level. Some jobs require a development degree in a specific development related area or a more general development studies degree although neither alone demonstrates that you can actually do development work. Knowledge about issues and international players, goals and targets is clearly helpful to put other work in context and to know what is needed and why. It can be a useful plus for any development job, showing your interest and commitment, alongside a required set of skills.

Practical courses are the most useful (except perhaps in academic appointments) and that is particularly true if the course includes project management and/or a good length placement or internship. A post-graduate degree is increasingly required for higher level jobs, particularly one concerned with policy rather than management, and is often a good choice to consider when transferring into the sector at intermediate level. While acquiring specific skills will be crucial to any job, an MA in Development will help to show that you are aware where and how these skills could best be used as well as countering any political or commitment question that might accompany you if you work presently in the commercial world. This is part of 'knowing the sector' and will (potentially) help.

The Development Studies Association has a guide to development related courses – short- and long-term: www.devstud.org.uk. A guide listing members of the Conference of Development Studies Centres (CDSC) is produced by the Institute of Development Studies: www.ids.ac.uk. An evening class, short course or part-time study may be a good alternative and provide you with adequate information and training. Distance learning can be explored through www.distancelearning.hobsons.com and courses at certificate, diploma and degree level are offered by the Open University (www.open.ac.uk) in areas such as 'Development Management'.

Coaching and Personal Advice

"In my experience… those with a friend, partner, priest, colleague or coach who will travel with them are far more likely to reach their goal, whatever that might be. The end result seems to be more about the quality of the journey than merely what you are offering. Who will encourage you and challenge you? If you can't identify someone who will be unconditionally objective, and you are serious about the future, you may give some thought to hiring a coach". [25]

[25] Claire Pedrick, Director, 3DCoaching: www.3dcoaching.com

Personal coaching or life coaching is akin to sports training – getting you ready for the race but not doing it for you. You need ability, skills, hard work and commitment. Coaching could help you to be realistic about where you are now, have a clearer picture of where you want to be, and begin to create strategies to get you there. There are many highly qualified professional coaches and you need to make sure the one you choose has had relevant experience of and/or an understanding of the peculiarities of Development rather than the commercial sectors 'overseas' work.

e>volve (www.wse.org.uk) written by Claire Pedrick is especially helpful if you are unsure whether a career in Development is right for you. It is the only online self-coaching course specifically for those thinking of entering the development sector. Claire has had 18 years experience working in development overseas and in recruitment for a UK development agency as well as in coaching. *e>volve* deals with some of the issues raised in this book and challenges you in 12 email sessions to do something about it. Our associate coaches can be found at: www.3dcoaching.co.uk, www.changebychoice.co.uk and www.kcoach.net.

Individual coaching may be right for you, especially if you want on-going help and support, and clarity about what to do to reach your goal. It will cost you money, and for some people a one-off talk dealing with specific or identified questions is enough. For these people we offer *One to One* consultations, which give an hour or more with a trained and experienced adviser who has worked overseas and been involved in training/recruiting/coaching/counselling etc. You will get a chance to send your questions in advance and theses will be researched before the interview. You will also have your CV scrutinised. A *One to One* may save you wasting your time going down blind alleys and following presumptions. Depending on what you want to spend, you could get some follow-up: see www.wse.org.uk 'advice' for more information.

You have no excuses now! You have learned about yourself and the sector. You have also learnt about jobs, ways in and skills. All that is left is the process.

So, how do you do it?

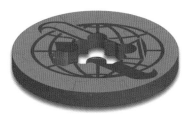

SECTION SIX:

Now Get Down To It

But First, Beware of Job Titles

Job titles may sound exciting but most don't convey any sense of the specific responsibility or technical knowledge that may be required. Job titles are only titles. You need more detailed information to check against your skills and experience. From our experience we know that people often mistakenly apply for jobs at a higher level of responsibility than their background warrants. The job description and particularly the person specification are the criteria you need to match; not the job title.

A Project Manager, for example, is a common job title but agencies using the title may mean something entirely different. There are number of points that you need to clarify before you consider applying for such a job.

- What project am I being asked to manage? Do I require specialist knowledge or skill? A health project may need the Project Manager to be a Doctor qualified in Public Health, for example.

- What is the scale of the responsibility? Is the project part of a larger country programme? If so, you will probably be reporting to the Programme Director and be responsible for staff. Is the programme one of many in a country? If so, there may also be another and higher level of Country Director to whom you will be responsible. Is it the only project in the country thus probably carrying greater responsibility than implied, or one of many similar projects in other countries with a line manager based at the NGO's HQ? How much control will the local manager be allowed?

- The scale of the responsibility may indicate the seniority of the job. The agency may expect previous overseas experience at a similar level, perhaps also country knowledge and maybe language fluency.

- If the job relates to a team, what is the size, what individual responsibility is expected and what is shared – is it really a 'team'?

These questions are just a few examples for you to consider. At all levels it is important to discover the real tasks and the proportion of time you will be using to do what you want.

Press advertising space is expensive and full details of the person specification don't appear in adverts due to limited space. Get further detailed information for jobs that you are interested in. When you have received and read this, consider whether you match the essential and desirable requirements and what proven experience you have to back up your application. Only apply if you meet all the essential criteria and be realistic in the level of seniority of job you apply for.

If you are thinking of applying for a job sometime in the future, it may be useful to build up a file on the range of experience agencies often require for particular jobs. Request details on the types of job you are interested in, or read all the details on the websites; you don't have to apply. If you don't have enough experience or the right skills now, you could obtain them through strategic planning.

Your portfolio of skills may mean you could apply for a range of different jobs. You are more than a job title, and jobs often involve more than the title!

Sources of Job Information

UK jobs are advertised in many ways: on an NGO's own website, in the press, through specialist portal websites and through recruitment agencies. Getting on to agency registers and databases may help; details of all these follow. The relevance of these many avenues to pursue will depend upon your personal circumstances and professional expertise. It would be a full-time job in itself to follow up all potential leads, so it is important to find the most suitable area to match your capabilities.

If you are looking for work overseas, there are also many ways you could begin and ideas follow below. A good way to see a selection of jobs and get a feel of the market before applying is through a three month subscription to our *Opportunities Abroad* (www.wse. org.uk). This selects jobs from many sources and specialises in publicising jobs that may not be widely advertised on major websites. It groups them in major areas: management, administrative, technical, education, health, etc. and includes entry level jobs.

The Internet

Many organisations first advertise their vacancies on their own web pages and prefer online or email applications. Even the most inexperienced job seeker needs intermediate computer ability to succeed in today's job market. *"Nearly 85 per cent of employers now use the Internet for recruiting."*[26]

With the establishment of global communications, wherever you are located, you now live in an information communication technology rich global world. Many people have the desire to work in a different country than their own and it is comparatively easy for anyone to find information and opportunities through development agencies websites and specialist listings. However, some jobs may have nationality restrictions built into the person specification and it is wise to ready the full details of an opportunity you may find on a foreign site.

The major advantage of Internet advertising is the low cost, with the added benefit of broadening the audience and increasing the chances of getting qualified applicants suitable for the job. It also means there is more competition as even more candidates are pursuing the same job.

However, there isn't one website that contains every available job opportunity and there are no easy solutions to finding work in your chosen field. There are large specialist development portals (such as reliefweb[27]) containing a vast array of information and in your search for work you need to be constantly visiting many sites.

Press Advertisements

This is an expensive option and consequently not used by all employers. Major players will use this method, partly to meet their own criteria of encouraging people from outside rather than allowing current employees to see an automatic 'career ladder'.

The following are the best sources of these traditional job advertisements.

In the national press such as *The Guardian* (Wednesday), *The Guardian Weekly, The Economist* and in professional journals. Each will also have a website.

In specialist newspapers and magazines:

- *International Career Employment Weekly* (www.internationaljobs.org) lists international jobs with the USA government, companies, intergovernmental agencies and voluntary organisations;

- *cinfo* have an online database of jobs (www.cinfo.ch) in French and German (and occasionally in English) providing vacancy notices for positions abroad and in Switzerland, these positions will be in the field of international cooperation mainly with Swiss agencies;

- *Third Sector* (www.thirdsector.co.uk) is a weekly magazine for professionals in the UK non profit sector with dedicated job sections on fundraising, finance and campaigning;

- *Opportunities Abroad* (World Service Enquiry www.wse.org.uk) is a monthly development jobs e-zine with vacancies in UK too, but most from international aid, development and faith based agencies.

Increasingly, many agencies offer regular vacancy bulletins or newsletters. Sign up to be added to their email list to receive regular updates of the latest jobs.

Special events and trade shows, such as *forum3*[28] may encourage employers to put jobs on vacancy notice boards.

Recruitment Agencies

Employment agencies and Management Recruitment Consultants recruit candidates for UK and some overseas jobs. Some of these agencies maintain databases of suitable candidates which they look at when vacancies occur. For speculative applications you may find Yellow Pages 'Employment Agencies' listing useful.

For overseas jobs, qualified and experienced professionals can contact The Expat Network (www.expatnetwork.com). They aim to help expatriates worldwide by linking members to overseas jobs. They produce country profiles, information on healthcare and schools, plus in-depth articles and industry reports on issues which affect expatriates. The Employment

---

[27] www.reliefweb.int

[28] forum3 is a specialist voluntary sector exhibition that takes place every October in London

Service Overseas Placing Unit provides information about a range of employment opportunities that exist in Europe via the EURES system (European Employment Services). You can find more information from your local Jobcentre Plus or look for jobs on www. jobcentreplus.gov.uk.

CharityJob (www.charityjob.co.uk), CR Search and Selection (www.crsearch.co.uk), Charity People (www.charitypeople.co.uk), Charity & Fundraising Appointments (www. cfappointments.com) and NFP JOBS (nfpjobs.netxtra.net) are some of the specialist voluntary sector job agencies, sometimes recruiting on behalf of some development agencies. Charity People also organise *Forum3* (www.forum3.co.uk), the UK's biggest recruitment and volunteering event for the non-profit sector at the Business Design Centre, Islington, in London, over a weekend in October.

Other agencies may be more specialised. For example, the Kage Partnership specialises in Fundraising and PR. These agencies include:

Charity Action Recruitment	www.c-a-r.org.uk
Charity Connections	www.charityconnections.co.uk
Eden Brown	www.edenbrown.com
Execucare	www.execucare.com
Harris Hill Ltd	www.harrishill.co.uk
Kage Partnership	www.kagep.com
Oxford HR Consultancy	www.oxfordhr.co.uk
Prospectus	www.prospect-us.co.uk
Skills for Causes	www.skillsforcauses.com
The Principle Partnership	www.tpp.co.uk

The specialist agency for recent graduates (not just in this sector) is www.prospects. ac.uk, a site with general advice too. And there are overseas specialists such as. Action Appointments (www.actionappointments.co.za) the only recruitment agency in South Africa which specialises exclusively in placements in the Development sector.

Registers

A number of agencies maintain emergency registers of skilled, experienced personnel who are available at short notice for short periods of time, to respond to a national or international crisis. RedR (http://onlinejobs.redr.org) maintain an emergency register, as do other agencies, such as Christian Aid (www.christian-aid.org.uk) and specialist agencies such as those with sniffer dogs useful in earthquake rescue. Applicants need to be highly qualified and skilled professionals with previous overseas relief experience. International Federation of Red Cross Red Crescent Societies (www.ifrc.org) maintains a register of skilled, experienced delegates who are available to work overseas on a fixed-term basis. Delegates are then seconded to work for the federation, the International Committee of the Red Cross (ICRC) or directly for the British Red Cross in the field when suitable positions arise.

Research what agencies do and you may find they have disaster management programmes as well as overseas and UK jobs. For example, in emergencies, Tearfund (www.tearfund.org) sends Disaster Management Teams that are made up of people with the following skills: community/public health Educators, water and sanitation Engineers, Team leaders, Project Managers, Finance officers/Accountants, Personnel Managers and Logisticians. Sometimes, the skills needed for some of these tasks are transferable from other jobs. Direct relief experience is desirable but not essential; a willingness to be an adaptable team member and previous overseas experience is essential.

In addition to emergency registers for relief workers, there are also a number of agencies that maintain registers or rosters of experienced personnel wanting to work overseas.

Action Against Hunger (www.aahuk.org) recruits throughout the year for a register of staff available for immediate overseas deployment. This register is referred to as the 'UK pool'. Staff within the UK pool will have been interviewed by the Human Resources department and the relevant Technical Advisor. AAH follow up on two references and gain confirmation that you are fit to work. Members of the pool and Action Against Hunger UK stay in regular contact to discuss potential work opportunities and an individual's availability.

The Commonwealth Fund for Technical Cooperation maintains a database that is used to identify suitable candidates for vacancies at Secretariat HQ in London, Technical Assistance assignments in developing Commonwealth countries and the Commonwealth Service Abroad Programme. For further details and to register visit the website: www.thecommonwealth.org.

Skillshare International will place your 'general recruitment programme' application on their register for a maximum period of 6 months: www.skillshare.org.

International Medical Corps need short-term staff available in some cases within 72 hours: www.imcworldwide.org.

Get on Databases

Databases are different from registers. Registers are for specifically skilled people who will be called upon in emergencies. Databases are suitable for people to submit their details for an automatic search when new jobs are notified. If you put in accountancy skills, for example, you will be informed if such jobs come up. Some will be searched by employers too.

You could try:

- www.crownagents.com;
- www.charitypeople.co.uk;
- www.devnetjobs.org;
- www.ids.ac.uk;
- www.reliefweb.int;
- http://uk.oneworld.net/jobs will send regular emails of new jobs
- http://jobs.guardian.co.uk (enter your details, attach a CV to get matching job details).

Specialised sites:

- Health workers   www.imcworldwide.org.uk;

- Finance jobs   www.mango.org.uk (also a register);

- Experienced people   www.devjobsmail.com (free list);

- Senior executives   www.cfappointments.com;

- Europe   www.cinfo.org (especially if you speak French);

- Non-NGO   email: expat_list-subscribe@topica.com.

Job Sources – A Summary and Some New Suggestions

In addition to registers and databases, there are general and specialist job lists. Good job sites include our own www.wse.org.uk – look at *Opportunities Abroad* – the only monthly up-dated listing via our web site, specialising in vacancies not often found on other searchable websites and including both secular and faith-based vacancies.

Another good place to start is www.waterberry.org. This site is targeted at young professionals who have a few years experience. Other general websites include the Gateway to International Development and Environment Jobs at www.devnetjobs.org and you can subscribe to their service by email.

VSO is the largest UK sending agency, the greatest number of jobs being in education. A two year job with them has good standing in the NGO world since it gives adequate experience, demonstrates your survivability and commitment, and shows you have used your skills; everything that is needed to progress in the sector. They have good preparation and personal support: www.vso.org.uk

General sites:

- www.alertnet.org (also information on emergencies);

- www.bond.org.uk;

- www.charityjob.co.uk – for jobs throughout the charity sector and not specifically in development;

- www.cinfo.ch (Swiss-based) has jobs for French and German speakers;

- www.devjobsmail.com;

- www.eldis.org;

- www.idealist.org (primarily USA non-profit jobs);

- www.internationaljobs.org lists US governmental and NGO jobs;

- www.internationalservice.org.uk;

- www.reliefweb.int especially if you have previous overseas experience.

Overseas agencies lists can be found at www.devdir.org and Cooperating for Cooperation (www.coop4coop.org) has a database searchable by name, nationality, country or activity.

Working for the United Nations is a common dream for people in many countries. As in many international agencies, language skills and local knowledge are important, and the UN tries to internationalise its staff. An overall picture can be found on www.unsystem. org and specialisms on: www.unicef.org (children); www.wfp.org (food programme); www.who.int (health); www.ohchr.org (human rights) and www.unhcr.org (refugees). A linked organisation is www.iom.int (migration). These are not direct job sites as most are advertised on https://jobs.un.org.

Experience gained the sector is often. The ExpatNetwork (www.expatnetwork.com) has many contacts and job details, but with all jobs consider whether it is helpful or relevant in gaining experience and skills and if they are transferable to the NGO sector.

Specialist sites include:

- Fundraising www.crsearch.co.uk;

- For ethical careers try www.ethicalcareersguide.co.uk or http://peopleandplanet.org;

- For microfinance www.microfinancegateway.org, or www.alternative-finance.org.uk and http://microfinancejobs.com. Details of a Microenterprise Innovation Project can be found at www.microlinks.org;

- For environmental jobs try www.environmentjob.co.uk and *Working with the Environment* by Tim Ryder and Deborah Penrith. www.nature.com/naturejobs widens this to more general nature related jobs;

- For human rights jobs look at Human Rights Watch www.hrw.org and www.hri.ca/ jobboard (mainly USA);

- Sustainable development work is advertised on www.environmentalcareer.com, www.environmentjob.co.uk, www.earthworks-jobs.com, www.greenbiz.com/jobs, www.greendirectory.net/jobs and www.sustainablebusiness.com/jobs;

- Health jobs can be found on many sites including Merlin www.merlin.org.uk, International Medical Corps (www.imcworldwide.org). www.aidsalliance.org has jobs and links for work in the HIV/AIDS sector;

- Feminist and women's sites are listed on www.awid.org. Though not all have jobs, they may lead to agencies that are worth contacting such as WOMANKIND Worldwide www.womankind.org.uk;

- www.international-alert.org/jobs and www.saferworld.org.uk have occasional jobs in conflict resolution, as does www.v4.crinfo.org (primarily USA-based);

- Mango exists to help aid agencies and NGOs to work more effectively by strengthening their financial management, and has details of jobs and internships www.mango.org.uk/recruitment;

- For academic jobs look at www.jobs.ac.uk and www.agcas.org.uk;

- www.comhlamh.org has lists of agencies and jobs from Irish NGOs as well as a workgroup to help people get involved. www.ideas-forum.org.uk offers the same for Scotland;

- General advice on jobs for Christians in development and mission can be found through Christians Abroad (www.cabroad.org.uk), www.christianvocations.org or www.oscar.org.uk. For Christian faith-based agencies working in health try the Christian Medical Fellowship, www.cmf.org.uk;

- Those with learning difficulties should try www.rkl.org.uk, and for other disabilities, www.disabilitytoolkits.ac.uk;

- CAF International has information on and directories of NGOs in India, South Africa, USA, Australia and parts of Eastern Europe. These are not job lists but provide a useful way to find out more information to network, www.cafonline.org. Try also www.devdir.org;

- www.interimsfd.com has short-term technical, training and project jobs and their magazine reviews employment opportunities;

- Teaching is one way of gaining regional experience and language skills (but preferably not in a commercially-oriented private school in a major city) try www.tefl.com.

Our *Guide to Volunteering for Development* gives details of 36 UK major agencies, detailing where they work and the skills they need, www.wse.org.uk.

Applying for Jobs

Personnel Officers or Human Resources staff have little time to peruse initial applications in detail. Those who do not meet the minimum requirements are excluded immediately, but the rest are also often examined fairly cursorily before short-listing.

Imagine you are working in Human Resources looking at applications…

50% do not even meet minimum requirements and are not even looked at.	Rejected
25% are not attractive enough in presentation to get further attention.	Rejected
With the right skills and presentation you might get here.	Selected for long list
Invited for interview. What will get you here?	Short-listed

Be realistic and do your research. Find out about the organisation advertising the job and don't add to your disappointment by applying unrealistically. Four major agencies reported the following numbers of applications.[29]

- Save the Children: 7300 enquiries, 2600 applications, 720 people interviewed for 220 vacancies.

- VSO (staff jobs, not overseas volunteers): 2200 applications for 93 vacancies.

- World Vision: 2500 enquiries, 325 applications, 20 appointed.

- DFID: 1800 applications for 45 vacancies for their APSO programme (now replaced with Fast Stream).

---

[29] Getting into International Development: first edition from SOAS.

Do's and Don'ts of Your Application

Both www.devjobsmail.com and http://jobsadvice.guardian.co.uk list common mistakes to avoid and make suggestions to get your application to the short-list stage.

Some Do's

- Do your homework on the organisation. Check its website, see what specialist terminology or jargon it uses. Check English and Welsh charity entries on the Charity Commission site, www.charitycommission.gov.uk. For Scottish charities, see The Office of the Scottish Charity Regulator, www.oscr.org.uk and Northern Ireland, the Department for Social Development, www.dsdni.gov.uk.

- Completely read the advert, web details or information. What do they really want? See if there are key words and use them to prove you can do the job.

- Answer all the questions and don't give information not requested.

- Be realistic – if they say they want an MSc, they mean it.

- Have someone else check your CV or form.

- Do a draft and get someone who knows you well to check it.

- Follow instructions for submitting applications.

- If you are asked for a personal statement, address the key areas in the person specification and inject a little of your own personality while remaining the kind of person the organisation would like to have. The Guardian suggests: "*The function of writing a personal statement is just to get you through the door. You are most likely to succeed in this by offering more evidence that you have the skills and qualities the employer is looking for.*"[30]

- Emails: realise that people will not open unexplained email attachments such as zipped files and use common file types such as doc, rtf or pdf.

- If you submit online, treat this with equal seriousness in spelling and grammar. This is not like an email to a friend. Be even more careful about using key words from the person specification as it may be searched electronically for applicants using certain key words.

Some Don'ts

- The main don't is very simple: if you don't have the minimum requirements of qualifications and experience, then don't bother!

- Don't keep applying to organisations that have said 'No'.

- Don't tell them what you think they should be doing.

- Don't use an email address which suggests stupidity, drugs, pornography or laziness.

- Don't use the email address of a spouse or friend as this may suggest you do not think or act independently or have appropriate IT skills.

---

[30] The Guardian – Jobs advice

It all seems common sense, but as someone who reads many applications, I know just how many don't keep to these very sensible rules!

Application Forms

Fashion changes and it now seems to be moving back to application forms rather than letters plus CVs. Oxfam is one organisation that asks you simply to list qualifications and jobs and then tell them why you should be considered for the job. Many of the ideas listed in the following sections need to be applied to what you write, but check what they want to know and never give unnecessary information.

- If using paper, copy the forms and have a rough attempt first; it will help to see what it looks like. First impressions count.

- Don't crowd the whole space with words. What you leave out here can emerge at interview.

- Fill in the form completely. Don't put 'see attached CV' or other notes, especially if you have been asked to fill in the form 'completely'. Multiple forms are annoying to interviewers anyway, so don't put them off even more. If you are asked for gender, age or ethnic details these should be on a separate form to monitor equal opportunities policy and should not influence decisions.

- Usually there will be sections on work experience, academic achievements, personal achievements, and specific questions or you may simply be asked why you want the job. Context, Action and Results is one suggested formula. Use this to answer specific questions such as describing a project or piece of work you have completed.

- Don't attach copies of certificates/qualifications unless requested and never send originals to organisations you do not know.

- Remember you need to fit the person specification even more than the job description. In this sector, who you are is important.

Job Descriptions and Person Specifications

A job description will usually explain the job title and list the main purpose, followed by key tasks. The job title itself may not be very informative. There may then be more detail, e.g. size of team or budget, etc. It is designed to get you interested and target the best candidates.

A person specification will usually deal more with work or technical experience and soft skills but it should not do so in a discriminatory way. It will be less general and more about the personal skills and experience needed to do the job rather than the tasks themselves. The skills will often be grouped into essential and desirable. Think how you match these and imagine an interviewer or employer looking at a table similar to this.

	Essential	Desirable
Education and training	✓	
Experience	✓	
Specialist skills and aptitudes		✓
Personal qualities	✓	
Other requirements (language, knowledge, etc.)		✓

They will be investigating if and how you match the criteria.

In your application, whether it's a form or cover letter and CV, you must match the essentials and desirables with examples. If you lack anything, then don't tell them; HR will work it out. Don't be creative in trying to making irrelevant experience fit. And never assume that HR will read between the lines to work out what experience you have; tell them!

Email applications

I receive many email applications and around 90% are speculative and have not checked the kind of people we are looking for. It is obvious that they have also been sent to hundreds of other recruiters so they are rejected without being read through. This is particularly true of emailed CVs that arrive with just a line of introduction. For example, I reject automatically any message subject title that just says 'My CV' or 'consider me for jobs you have advertised'. Nowadays, there will be the suspicion such a brief message is spam or may contain a virus.

If the recruiter has asked for an email application, check the details of what they require. Type the subject as specified, or use the job title or reference number and, of course, ensure it reaches them by the closing date (and time).

Remember also:

- Ensure that only one email 'sent to' address appears at the top. Many will reject it if you have also sent it to a hundred other organisations, because you clearly have no interest in a specific job;

- Don't use a picture file or other attachment that takes time to download; you will not impress anyone;

- Don't include a photo as it introduces a possible element of discrimination;

- Internet connections can go wrong so don't leave it to the last minute any more than you would for a postal application.

Increasingly, online applications are used by NGOs and other recruiters. Not all of them are sophisticated forms and you may have to complete it at one go, so it is worth printing it off and giving yourself time to think about it before your start typing. Be careful when pressing 'enter' as on some online forms pressing this key can submit applications before completion.

Some electronic forms may pick up key words to help identify people for further consideration, so without being too obviously slavish to the person specification or job description, try to identify the key words in the skills needed for the job and use them in your application.

www.selectsimulator.com is linked to the Association of Graduate Careers Services (www.agcas.org.uk) and might help. It has a practice online application form with explanatory notes and is recommended by many university careers offices and it explains why employees use them and how to prepare.

Speculative Approaches

Few agencies welcome speculative applications. Many have neither the time nor the staff to deal with the deluge of irrelevant international enquiries. Before emailing, calling and writing to every agency you know, first:

- research what they do;
- find out if they are recruiting staff and, if so;
- what skills do they need?

Speculative applications can only be fruitful if you establish in advance whether the agencies you contact have vacancies for your skills. An agency's annual report, website, general publicity or books on working overseas will provide background information about the area of the agency's work and the skills it may recruit for. After your research, write briefly, stating simply what you have done and what you can offer; that is, what your expertise is. A speculative approach needs to be short and relevant to their needs; this is not the time to ramble, include referees or write your life story – Human Resource staff are busy people. You may need some practical help with a speculative job search and we can help you formulate a strategy through our *One to One* service or by putting you in touch with a career coach.

The critical factors are to contact the relevant person and to keep your enquiry short and to the point.

Improve Your CV

Pity the poor Human Resources person ploughing through hundreds of applications and CVs. How are you going to make reading yours take more than a few seconds of valuable time? Many employers have their own application forms and for them the covering letter will help (see below), but, where requested, a good CV is essential, and the analysis you need to do to create it will also be useful for completing the application forms. You need to see it as simply a device to get you an interview, and for the moment think how others will want to see you. You need to be able to expand on claims of skills, explain any gaps and show how what you have done relates to the job you are seeking.

Which Kind of CV?

There are two basic CV formats: chronological and functional (also called skills-based).

The chronological is the traditional format and that is partly because it fits with older employment patterns of people progressing through single or similarly related employment fields. It shows how you have learned and been promoted and so are ready for the next step. It shows maturity and commitment and is often the easiest to read. Employment records will be quite detailed, with the most recent jobs listed first and expanded upon more than older ones. Academic records will be the same but in less detail and any further sections on interests and voluntary activity can be flexible to fit the job being applied for. This kind of CV is usually less helpful if you are changing sectors or have employment gaps, and can sometimes seem repetitive and therefore unattractive.

A functional CV concentrates on achievements and transferable skills rather than where a person has worked or the precise job done. It is perhaps becoming more popular because it fits with modern employment patterns, where people move jobs more frequently. It would begin with key skills, then academic achievements followed by a much shorter list of employment. It allows you to emphasise a wider dedication to the sector, if you have been in it, as well as giving you a choice of which skills and past achievements to concentrate on that fit the new job. You need to have confidence that what you have done is transferable. Functional CVs can also be used with care if application forms are requested rather than a detailed CV. Sections can be cut and pasted, but always check for relevance.

One CV advice page[31] suggests that some employers maybe suspicious because these functional resumés and CVs can be used to cover up bits of failure and require a bit more work from the reader to find out what you've done. That probably depends on the opening statement which should show real skills and experience rather than boasting how wonderful you are.

Whatever you do, don't mix both formats. It can be very confusing to the recruiter or interviewer. In other words, don't put a detailed chronological job list with a skills summary. If you feel the chronological list does not bring out your skills, even if you are moving up in the same sector, but have not done all you are capable of and can prove you can do, then don't expand it but change to the functional format. Helpful advice on this can be found on www.charitypeople.co.uk under 'career advice', and we offer a specialist CV service at wse which will help you gain clarity on the art of writing your CV. Full details of our CV service can be found on our website at wse.org.uk.

CV Skills Analysis

As noted previously in 'What NGOs are looking for', the first determining factor in choice of personnel is skills; no job is possible without them, even if that has to be demonstrated by how you can transfer existing skills and develop new ones. Only then will the other factors come into play such as commitment and evidence that you will last the course. So you must be able to show that you can match the person specification or fit the other clues they give on the kind of person they want. A skills analysis may help, but in the end, it is how you make your view of yourself match what they want and what you feel confident in doing that is important. The following skills analysis may give you new ideas, but you have to feel confident to present yourself in a way which will convince people that you are the best available.

---

[31] See www.devjobsmail.com

When doing your own analysis, try dividing your skills into groups; these will be based on your experience. One such breakdown of skills is: specialist, general, self-reliance, and people skills. Other breakdowns might group either the first two, middle two or last two (self-reliance and people) together. Furthermore, some skills could be placed in a different area according to the job. For example, a foreign language is a people skill which makes it more likely that you can relate across cultures. But for some jobs it may be asked for as a specialist skill so you can hit the ground running by having a relevant language needed in a particular country. Similarly, team work skills could be presented either as an ability to work cooperatively, or as a specialist form of leadership. There is no single way, just make the list and then divide it according to what seems to fit their job. Online skills assessment programmes are listed in the section 'Do you know your skills?'.

However, the first step is clearly to list what you can do – the skills you have used or acquired – obvious and hidden. The technical or specialist part will be easiest: medical, social work, engineering, education, finance, agricultural, IT, etc. Within these there will clearly be particular experiences or qualifications that will be needed such as tropical health or agriculture, social worker with experience of working with the abused, specialist water Engineer, etc.

That analysis of the specialist part of your past work experience will make you suitable for interview, and supporting skills are what will get you into the final few to be interviewed. For these, your list of skills will help, especially if these can be used in a constructive and positive way in application forms, CVs or accompanying or covering letters, whichever are asked for.

CV Skills Portfolio

Some ideas now to start you to thinking about what you are good at in addition to technical skills.

Basic

The skills often asked for, or required to be shown at the interview will include: adaptability, cultural sensitivity, willingness to listen and learn, sense of humour, ability to work in a team. Also in this general list are: determination, resilience, consultative decision-making, ability to cope in isolation (specifically for overseas jobs), ability to learn languages, reconciliation skills.

Personal

Much of the list here can be used in other sections, depending on the job: supportive, imaginative, open-minded, visionary, constructive, dynamic, tolerant, emplastic, reflective, persuasive, proactive, self-starter, self-reliant, intuitive, initiator, motivated, keen learner, forward thinker, planner, creative, practical, astute, versatile, accurate, methodical, thorough, organiser, risk-taker, reliable, conscientious.

Communication

This is both in the way you communicate and your particular uses of communication skills. These may be: mediating, networking, initiating, advising, facilitating, liaising, and negotiating. Uses that communication skills have been put to could include, advising, lecturing, preaching, presenting, publicising, training and writing.

Management

There is an extensive list here, but project management is the aim of many development workers: managing people, motivating colleagues, exercising diplomacy, administering, strategic planning, appraising, evaluating, minuting meetings, analysing, monitoring, prioritising, problem solving, logical decision making, lateral thinking. Other specific people skills may be useful but are perhaps better described as specialist or 'technical': coaching; counselling; mentoring; accompaniment.

Linked with the above there may be specific groups of people you have applied these skills to, and these need to be mentioned: community groups, ethnic minorities, children or other age groups, refugees/asylum seekers, disabled, marginalised, etc.

Finance

Finance is often important as a subsidiary skill, even if not in its own right: basic bookkeeping, budgeting, technical control. This area also has specific 'technical' skills that are often the core of the job: accountancy, fundraising, marketing.

Presentation

This can be an important area for small NGOs in particular: advocacy, campaigning, marketing, and reporting. Behind all these can be research and analysis.

Information

While this general area overlaps (as do many others), there are specific skills to mention: information management, database, spreadsheet, website, DTP, word processing. (Note: don't overemphasise details of these unless it is a specialist IT job).

Grouping skills

Having examined your skills and perhaps found new ones, how do you group them together? This section helps you to group them to help compile your CV. Some skills appear in more than one area and their position for you will depend on their ultimate importance in the job. For example, a language skill, in a job in French-speaking Africa would be a necessary specialist skill. For other jobs it is a people skill, showing interest in peoples sufficient to learn their language and therefore helping you to relate cross-culturally. The following four sections may themselves not be suitable for all jobs and, as already said, people and personal could be amalgamated.

In a CV, these skills need to be amplified, using the active words listed in the following 'Do's and Don'ts' section. For example, not 'fundraiser', but "increased funding by 35% to £56k in two years".

One suggestion for grouping skills.

- **people**
  List skills that show how you relate to others (centred on the job).
  Interpersonal: culturally sensitive, listener, tactful, empathic.
  Team working: cooperative, coordinator, facilitator.
  Leadership: initiator, innovator, organiser, manager, trainer.
  Communication: trainer, teacher, communicator, language skills, cross-cultural, interviewing.

Project management: (put in specialist if in job title) practical, creative, manager, analytical, finance.

■ Personal

Note differences here from 'people skills'.

Commitment: Show issues important to you, plus evidence from organisations or projects supported.

Voluntary work: List full- and part-time, including membership, advocacy, campaigning, causes and organisations.

Cross-cultural: Overseas and UK experience.

Personal: conscientious, reliable, welcoming, accepting of difference, listener.

■ Specialist

Here put the skills essential to the job.

Technical: engineering, medicine, language, accounting, fundraising, marketing, programme management.

Specific: Within those general technical skills note specific experience, e.g. Two years managing HIV awareness programme in...; managed team budget of...

■ General/practical

As with others, these categories need to be selected to meet the person specification.

Numeracy: logical, problem solver, quick thinker, analytical.

Office Skills: bookkeeping, accountancy, IT (huge detail only if specific to job), data management.

Communication: Writing, speaking, photography, radio.

Business: enterprising, competitive, instigator.

Some CV Do's and Don'ts

Do

Many applicants will have the same degree/academic or similar work history. Therefore ask yourself what makes you shine out? Motivation is one factor, but if your CV shows relevant skills and personal information you may at least get beyond the first stage. Some hints.

■ Keep it short. It must be no more than 2 sides of A4. If you need to show a breadth of experience (e.g. in health jobs where often there is frequent job change and re-training) or for an academic job where publications and papers are relevant, add as an appendix.

■ Make an impact but don't be too eccentric.

■ Make it look neat and ordered. Pay attention to the white space as well as the text.

■ A couple of lines of introduction (a profile) about your skills are fine. Make sure you use the first person: I am, I have, and not "Sarah has gained..." Write about yourself!

■ Use facts to back up the claims. Give the precise job title rather than "worked in conservation". Say "raised £X, an increase of X%" rather than "successful fund-raiser". Show your commitment and experience as well as ability.

- Check the person specification. In this sector, often this is more important than the job description so if you don't match the person specification then don't apply.

- Use a standard or 'master' CV as the basis of your CV, but doctor it for each application; generic CVs don't work.

- Always use reverse chronology; latest things first.

- Spell-check and look at the detail; check hyphens and dashes and full stops.

- Give more detail of the latest information, places, date, the highest qualifications, research topics/subject areas in degrees, emphasising bits similar to the job being applied for.

- List training, again concentrating on latest and relevant parts; show you are keeping up to date. Where directly relevant, include major conferences or seminars. Referees: probably best to say "references available". If they are asked for, make sure your referees know you have used them.

- Spell-check again or better still, get someone to read it through.

- Include voluntary activities and interests when relevant to the job.

- Include your soft skills.

Emphasise transferable skills; use active verbs and be positive.

achieved	established	produced
built	implemented	provided
campaigned	improved	raised
controlled	initiated	recruited
coordinated	managed	represented
created	monitored	resourced
designed	organised	supervised
directed	planned	trained etc
energised	presented	

Don't

- Don't give date of birth, marital status, children, age, status, personal statistics, faith or nationality (unless the latter is needed to prove you have a right to work). These can be seen as discriminatory and should not be asked for unless the job has a specific need (e.g. on some women's issues, some faith-based agencies).

- Don't use colour, fancy scripts, graphics or photos. These may not photocopy well or be transferable to potential interviewers.

- Don't give your present work telephone number if it is difficult to speak or you haven't yet said you are leaving.

- Don't leave unexplained blanks. If unemployed, say "job searching" or even better, fill it with voluntary activities. Otherwise what were you doing? In prison, long-term illness, or just lazing around? All sorts of assumptions might be made.

- Don't use an email address that may be misinterpreted.

- Don't lie – discovery will mean instant dismissal.

And Additionally

Remember all the time to emphasise your skills. Guidance can be found at www.3dcoaching.com/career_coaching/writing_your_cv.phtml and at www.handsoncv.co.uk/writeacv.aspx.

More details can also be found on www.awid.org and www.jobhuntersbible.com (both have a US bias). Other sites, with a commercial jobs bias, are www.totaljobs.co.uk, www.fish4.co.uk and www.monster.co.uk. www.agcas.org.uk is especially useful to recent graduates and has CV writing as part of its career management skills page.

The Guardian website http://jobsadvice.guardian.co.uk has a link to the Fuller CV service which offers a free CV review on www.thefullercv.com. Any search engine will bring up a huge list for 'Free CV' but most of these will give a basic service and offer to do more for a fee, and hope you will want other services from them. Most will lean towards what is needed in the commercial sector. One of the reasons for a switch back to completed application forms being again considered far more important than a CV is this 'professionalisation' of CVs, they are all part of a pattern, too similar and will be recognised immediately by recruitment personnel. Yours needs to be individual and present the real you.

Need some personal help? The career advice service CVCheck of wse at www.wse.org.uk will help you to get your CV right for the Development sector.

Covering Letter

Check if a covering letter is required in addition to an application form and CV. If it's not excluded, this can be a useful way to ensure your application is looked at. Make it as personal as possible, related to the kind of job available and the kind of person desired.

- Say why you are interested in the organisation, the particular job, and how you heard of it.

- Highlight your strengths and accomplishments and show briefly how they are relevant to the organisation and job in question. Check the person specification for this.

- Re-state your interest and provide contact information. Say you look forward to hearing from them.

- Don't repeat your CV text, although you can refer to it, emphasising relevant specific skills or experience.

- Keep it less than a full page on plain white paper and look at how the text is spaced. If you are asked to handwrite the letter, ensure that it is legible!

- Refer to any previous contact (letter, telephone).

- Use the name of the person mentioned in the advert or letter to you, and use Mr/Ms etc. If the name has no title then it is okay to use any given first name.

Never use a standard letter – it has to be specific to the job. Be sure to spell-check and proof read before you send. Ask someone to check that you have neither overdone it nor been too modest. The www.awid.org 'Getting a Job' page is valuable for all but particularly for women, whom, it suggests, often undersell themselves.

Interview Skills   ›

"Hard skills get an applicant an interview but soft skills will get that person a job. "[32]

This quotation comes from a medical site but the truth applies elsewhere. Hard skills are specific and can generally be learned and will be shared by most coming to the interview. Interviewees will fit the 'job description' or "minimum skills" outline. If not they would have already been rejected. A nurse will have hard skills as a result of training, but bedside manner is part of who s/he is. Interviewers may therefore test soft skills with questions about how you expressed or worked through a particular incident or period of work. If you say you are a good team player in your CV then can you answer the question on how to cope or deal with difficult individuals in a team? Short examples are needed; long life stories are not helpful. There may be clues to the questions you may be asked in the person specification.

Some of the interviewers may probably have to work with you, and you have to appear to be the kind of person they would want as a colleague.

Be sensible; think about what you wear, check where you are going and how long it will take, and don't be late. If you are delayed, call them to see if they can see you later. On meeting shake hands and smile, be attentive to the interviewers. Don't smell of alcohol, cigarettes or garlic. Sit straight and be confident: they have asked you in because they are interested in meeting you! Don't be rude about your present employer as it will show you can be disloyal and it also be a small world! Do your homework on the organisation, its website, publications, etc.

Prepare. Think of how you might answer the following.

- Why do you want this job?
- What is especially attractive about this job?
- What do you think are your strengths/weaknesses?
- Give an example of how you have approached… (a common issue in this area of work).
- What do you think of….? (For example, government policy changes in this area, recent press publicity on the subject).
- What skills do you have that would convince us you are the right person?
- Tell us how you work with other people?

Some other points to consider.

- Everyone will claim to be hard-working and motivated. Think of examples unique to you.

[32] www.medhunters.com/articles/softskills

- Greet the interviewers (and shake hands), and thank them after the interview for their time.

- Have some pre-prepared questions but don't jump in on salary or already booked holidays. Instead ask about the development plans of the organisation.

- Use any time they give you in "Do you have any questions to ask us?" to emphasise any skill or relevant topic that you feel has not come out in the interview and by asking about on-going training, personal development, etc. This gives a clear impression of commitment.

- Answer the questions and also try to draw their attention to why they should employ you; emphasise identified skills.

- Practice your interview technique!

- Avoid "you know", "like" etc., as well as too many "ers" and "ums".

- Be positive and don't exaggerate. Take ownership of the job and say "when" and "I would" and not "I think" and "if".

- On some issues you may need to show your commitment, and then it is also acceptable to say what other people think.

- Use action words you used on your application; reinforce your capabilities.

You may be called to a second interview, or asked to complete a questionnaire or test. Don't be too worried since you will not be expected to be perfect in your answers; it may be a confirmation of details to be followed by an offer.

A web search will produce many sites that claim they will help you with interviews. Like CV sites, there is often a charge for anything beyond basic advice. One useful UK site is www.job-interview.net which has a seven part 'Interview Success Plan'. See also London University, www.careers.lon.ac.uk, where there are pages of ideas of questions you may be asked with suggested answers and possible questions for you to give them, such as: What training could I expect? How has the vacancy arisen? Who will I be working most closely with? And, don't forget there are many helpful books on interviews.

If you make relevant, good applications then you will be called in for interview. If you are the best candidate they may offer you the job. But remember, interviews are a two way process; you can choose if it's right for you.

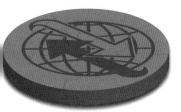

SECTION SEVEN:
Any more help?

We hope that the information in this book has helped you make sense of your Development puzzle. Did all your pieces fit? Or, are you missing a piece?

At World Service Enquiry we know that many people are interested in working in Development but only a few reach their goal. We are the only specialist information and advice charity not recruiting for ourselves, and we are here to help you.

For some, trying to find relevant information and the sheer amount of it can be overwhelming. Globally there are literally thousands of agencies and organisations seeking staff or offering voluntary placements. Where you fit in will depend on your experience, circumstances, resources and abilities.

If you are experiencing difficulties with finding or applying for a job, we are able to help you through our practical vocational advice service, *One to One*. The process looks at your CV, qualifications, experience, motivation and personal circumstances and starts to suggest practical ways for you to move forward to your ideal job. We have advised new graduates right through to senior executives seeking to transfer their skills into the development sector as well as coaching overseas development workers on three continents. If you want some pragmatic sensible advice then consider talking to one of our advisers in a *One to One*.

Opportunities Abroad is Europe's only job e-zine featuring development related jobs from aid, emergency, development and faith agencies and professional recruiters. It specialises in jobs not widely advertised elsewhere and on UK agencies' and entry level jobs.

Our *CV Check* service is specially geared to the Development sector and will certainly help you to gain clarity and get your CV right.

We also offer a unique email coaching service called *e>volve*, through our website. Based on the most common issues raised in our One to One service, *e>volve* offers a cheaper alternative to the personal One to One but is not interactive. Over eight weeks you receive twelve emails that will question, inform and encourage you into action to find work within the Development sector.

Full details of our publications and services can be found on our website www.wse.org.uk.

Many successful people get some practical support and encouragement while job hunting. If you feel you need longer term support, encouragement and the knowledge of a development sector expert, we recommend you employ the services of a coach. The coaches and advisors known to us can be found at www.changebychoice.co.uk, www.3dcoaching.com and www.kcoach.net and all offer a free introductory session.

Other Resources

The *Guide to Volunteering for Development* from wse (www.wse.org.uk) is a guide about being involved in volunteering either at home or overseas and lists over 350 voluntary agencies. You can purchase the most recent print copy through the website.

The series of 'How to Books' are helpful: e.g. *World Volunteers, Working with the Environment, Taking a Career Break, Internships in the USA, Green Volunteers*, etc. (www. howtobooks.co.uk).

The Directory of Social Change's *International Development Directory* (www.dsc.org.uk) is a useful overall source of information.

London University's School of Oriental and African Studies, SOAS, have a guide, *Getting into International Development* that you can buy from The Careers Group, www.careers. lon.ac.uk, though much of it is a survey of organisations. VSO's, *Return Volunteer's Guide* also has some useful information.

The independently published *Ethical Careers Guide* (www.ethicalcareersguide.co.uk) is a comprehensive guide to a wider range of possibilities which are a possible 'way in' to the Development sector or a way of working at similar world issues.

There are many general sites on development. www.dev-zone.org and www.devstud.org. uk link development studies departments, and offer resources as well as jobs. www.eldis. org has regular updates on development issues, conference papers, etc.

The New Internationalist produces a series of paperbacks on subjects related to Development from *International Development* to *World Poverty, Globalization, HIV/AIDS, International Migration* and *Water* and many others.

There is a huge amount of information, including technical articles, available online from the British Library of Development Studies at Sussex University, http://blds.ids.ac.uk.

Lastly

If you are confused after reading this book, or unsure about what to do, which career path to take, or if you are looking for work or want to transfer your skills, *What Color is Your Parachute? A Practical Manual for Job-hunters and Career Changers*, (Richard N. Bolles ISBN 1580087272) would be very helpful. *The What Color is Your Parachute* website can be found at www.jobhuntersbible.com.

Appendix A

Wheel of Life

Ann Mold from Change by Choice (www.changebychoice.co.uk) suggests the 'Wheel of Life' may help you discover the areas of your life where you need to pay attention.

Draw a line in each segment to represent how important each is in your life at the moment (graduated 0 –10 from the inside to outside of the spokes) and then ask yourself what 10/10 would be in each category.

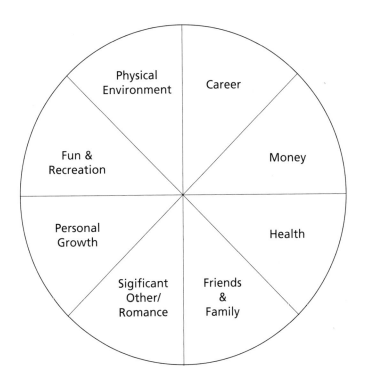

When that is finished, ask yourself:

- What are my priorities?
- What are the key issues I need to address?
- Where do I excel?
- What must I develop, study, practise or learn?

If some of these are important to you, a career outside development may be more relevant especially if the finished line is very jagged. Ann would be happy to discuss your results with you email:ann@changebychoice.co.uk or visit www. changebychoice.co.uk.

Appendix B

Local Groups

It is always useful to be part of a local group; for networking, learning current issues, practising and developing skills.

Details of local charities can be found through your local Volunteer Bureau as well as www.do-it.org.uk. In addition, you may find opportunities advertised in the local press. Many national NGOs also encourage people to join local groups, the following list is a small sample of those:

Action for Southern Africa	www.actsa.org
AFS	www.afsuk.org
Amnesty International	www.amnesty.org.uk
ATD Fourth World	www.atd-uk.org
CAFOD	www.cafod.org.uk
Campaign Against Arms Trade	www.caat.org.uk
Christian Aid	www.christian-aid.org
Friends of the Earth	www.foe.co.uk
Greenpeace	www.greenpeace.org.uk
Interserve	www.interserve.org
Jubilee Debt Campaign	www.jubileedebtcampaign.org.uk
Nicaragua Solidarity Campaign	www.nicaraguasc.org.uk
One World Week	www.oneworldweek.org
Oxfam	www.oxfam.org.uk
Save the Children	www.savethechildren.org.uk

- Online shopping is also available from One Village (www.onevillage.org) who offer a range of fair trade products.

Use your Powers and Liberties

- Invest your money with ethical investment companies.

- Join and be active in a political party, trade union or lobbying group.

- If you are a shareholder, insist on just dealings within companies.

- Support and be active in campaign organisations such as the World Development Movement (www.wdm.org.uk) or support the Jubilee Debt Campaign (www.jubileedebtcampaign.org.uk). Write to and lobby MPs and MEPs. Local MP information is available from your library or www.parliament.uk.

- MEPs can be contacted through The European Parliament Office at www.europarl.org.uk.

- Support and uphold human rights. Be active in organisations like Anti-Slavery International (www.antislavery.org) or Survival International (www.survival-international.org).

- People and Planet (www.peopleandplanet.org) organises a student campaign network taking action on world poverty, human rights and the environment.

- Be involved in or organise events for One World Week (www.oneworldweek.org) that each October focuses on a specific theme to raise awareness. Challenge and educate others within your community.

- Mount exhibitions, show relevant DVDs to community groups, run workshops, do slots on local radio, write to the local paper, write a blog.

- Encourage your family, friends or work colleagues to join in, for example, CAFOD's Fast Days.

- Be involved in National Fairtrade Fortnight which takes place during the first two weeks of March every year organised by the Fairtrade Foundation.

- Lobby for fair trade coffee at work for example, and shop at pre-Christmas Fair Trade Fairs such as WorldFair (www.worldfair.org.uk).

- Be active in a campaign focused on an issue or region.